Death Wishes?

Death Wishes?

The Understanding and Management of Deliberate Self-Harm

H. G. Morgan
Professor of Mental Health
University of Bristol

Honorary Consultant Psychiatrist
Avon Area Health Authority

JOHN WILEY & SONS LIMITED
Chichester · New York · Brisbane · Toronto

Copyright © 1979 by John Wiley & Sons Ltd.

Library of Congress Cataloging in Publication Data:

Morgan, Howard Gethin.
    Death wishes?

    Bibliography: p.
    Includes Index.
    1. Suicide.   I. Title.   II. Title: Deliberate self-harm.
RC569.M67   616.8′5844   79-1044

ISBN 0 471 27591 3

Photosetting by Thomson Press (India) Ltd., New Delhi and
printed by The Pitman Press, Bath.

CONTENTS

ACKNOWLEDGEMENTS

I am grateful to my clinical and research colleagues for sharing with me the many problems of patient care which have been presented to us in Bristol during the last ten years. Such collaboration provided much of the basis on which I have been able to develop the various ideas concerning self-harm which are embodied in this book. I am particularly grateful for the constant help and support which has been provided by Professor D. Russell Davis.

Much of the research data concerning our own studies of self-harm were collected and analysed by Helen Pocock, Sue Pottle, and Jackie Barton, with the secretarial help of Noreen Iles. Miss Ethel Duncan, Mrs. A. Morris, and Mrs. J. Williams of the University of Bristol Department of Community Medicine kindly undertook the necessary computer analysis. Dr. C. J. Burns-Cox, Consultant Physician, Frenchay Hospital, collaborated with us on part of the project. Financial support was provided by the Medical Research Council.

I am also grateful to Dr. A. J. Rowland, Community Physician, Bristol Health District (Teaching) for allowing me access to his own research data concerning suicide mortality statistics in Bristol. Access to inquest reports was possible by permission of Mr. Seymour Williams, the Bristol City Coroner. Dr. Ian Pierce James, Consultant Psychiatrist, kindly allowed me to use illustrations concerning self-laceration (Figure 11) devised from his own research material.

INTRODUCTION

The aim of this book is to consider the causes, management, and prevention of those forms of behaviour which may be included under the general category 'acute deliberate self-harm'.

A clear distinction is made between fatal self-harm or suicide, which is considered in Part I, and all episodes of acute deliberate self-harm which are non-fatal, these being dealt with separately in Part II. There is considerable debate regarding the justification for categorizing self-harm in this way, and such a classification is by no means a perfect one. Some who kill themselves do so accidentally, whilst a proportion who survive had probably intended to commit suicide but misjudged the situation. Apart from such uncertainties regarding motivation, there is also a great deal of overlap in the two groups with regard to personal and social characteristics of individuals in each. Nevertheless, major differences exist between the two, particularly from the epidemiological point of view, and it would seem important to separate the two groups in a work of this kind; only by doing so can we discern factors which are pertinent to either but which may not be relevant to both. It must be emphasized from the start, however, that a classification which depends upon whether self-harm results in death or survival should not be taken to imply that the two groups are mutually exclusive in all ways.

It is a basic assumption throughout that we need to have command of the relevant facts before it becomes possible to formulate theories of causation. These in turn permit discussion of the assessment and management of persons who are at increased risk of deliberate self-harm and who may present to us in various ways.

At all points an attempt has been made to achieve a synthesis between the epidemiological–sociological–statistical approach, on the one hand, and the individual clinical one, on the other. A rational view of deliberate self-harm can only be based on an adequate knowledge of both.

Although a considerable amount of reference is made in the text to the findings from our Bristol studies, these are discussed fully in the light of other recent research developments from elsewhere. In this way an attempt has been made to bring together a wide body of information which is not always easily or immediately available.

The chapter headings in the two parts of the book are similar but not exactly analogous, owing to certain minor differences in emphasis of approach towards suicide and non-fatal self-harm. The first chapter in Part I is a historical review of suicide and attempts to provide an appropriate perspective for subsequent consideration of the problem of deliberate self-harm as it presents itself today.

Part I

SUICIDE

1

HISTORICAL REVIEW

We are unlikely to reach an objective understanding of suicide without a historical perspective. Before proceeding to present-day considerations of its incidence, causes, treatment, and prevention a very brief review is therefore necessary with regards to the way it has occurred in various societies in the past. Because information is so much more easily available we will be concerned primarily with the history of suicide in Western civilizations. For a more detailed consideration the reader is referred to the works of Choron (1972), Dublin (1963), and Rosen (1971), to which this present account is greatly indebted.

Suicide seems to have occurred in all groups and societies in which there is surviving documentary evidence and its precise significance has always puzzled man. The reasons for suicide have reflected the particular social conditions which applied at any particular time. It appears to have been infrequent in the Jews of Antiquity and when it did occur the most common reason was to escape the consequence of political or military defeat. In Greek and Roman times the common circumstances surrounding suicide were again military or political, such as the need to maintain honour or avoid capture, humiliation, and shameful death. Occasionally suicide would be prompted by zealous loyalty such as amongst soldiers when their leader died or in the practice of suttee in India whereby a wife would commit suicide following the death of her husband. During the period between the sixth century B.C. and the first century A.D. many professed a profound pessimism about life, presumably prompted by its barbarity and uncertainty. Both the Greek and Roman Stoics professed a contempt for the human condition and a resentment against the world and the self: their teaching explicitly condoned suicide, particularly when it was on behalf of one's country, for the sake of friends, or because of intolerable pain, mutilation, or incurable disease.

3

4

The early Christians frequently chose voluntary martyrdom: in fact they did so with an enthusiasm which was often a cause of embarrassment to their oppressors. There was of course considerable inducement in their religious belief that they would proceed to life in the next world, achieving remission of sin in the process of becoming a blood witness to Christ. Suicide had an intense fascination for the Christians during the first three centuries A.D., and some such as the Donatists sought out death by provoking others as well as by their own hands.

Mass suicide has occurred at regular intervals throughout the centuries, usually when a sect was persecuted and its very existence threatened: not surprisingly, deeply held religious convictions have frequently appeared to be the group's unifying force. In A.D. 74 the 960 Jewish Zealot defenders at Masada killed themselves after three years of siege by the Roman Legions of Titus. They preferred to perish rather than fall into the hands of the Romans and it may be significant that a belief in life after death had at that time become widespread among the Jewish people. There are also much later examples of mass suicide by Jewish minorities under persecution, e.g. at Mainz, York, Verdon, and Nemirov (Ukraine) during the eleventh to fourteenth centuries, death being preferred to forced conversion, torture, rape, and massacre. Amongst the thirteenth century French heretic Christian adherents of the Catharic heresy, the Albigenses, suicide by the 'undura' or voluntary fast was common. Many of the seventeenth century Russian Schismatics who clung to the Old Faith after the reform of the Russian Orthodox Church preferred mass suicide in crowded churches rather than a change in their way of life and allegiance to their faith. Clearly, throughout the centuries communities with a strong sense of internal allegiance have tended to see suicide as the only acceptable solution when severe persecution has threatened their very existence as a group. This phenomenon has continued to occur up to the recent past in the present century: suicide was common amongst a Cossack community in 1945 when it was faced with a forcible return to Russia against which it had fought during World War II. It certainly appears from historical descriptions of suicide that social forces which bind the individual to his peers or which contribute to the cohesion of a community can be of paramount importance, and self-destructive behaviour may result when they are severely threatened. Such historical examples can still help us to understand the social mechanisms which may play a part in suicides of today.

Suicide appears always to have evoked some kind of response from the community in which it occurs. Attitudes towards it have varied considerably both with time and from one society to another. They have been characterized by their arbitrariness and ambivalence, even when couched in strongly religious terms, giving the impression of being related more to expediency with regards to the prevailing social climate rather than having any absolute basis. No matter what the point in history, there is evidence of debate concerning the nature of suicide, as to whether it is a sin or is justifiable, and, if the latter, under what circumstances it may be committed. Socrates (470–399 B.C.) summed up man's resistance to suicide when he disdainfully refused to resort to it: 'There is a doctrine whispered in secret that man is a prisoner who has no right to open the door and run away: this is a great mystery which I do not quite understand' (Russell, 1946).

Such uncertainty both with regards to the nature of death and its sequelae must undoubtedly have held many back from suicide even when their lives had become otherwise intolerable. The early Christian doctrine appears to have triggered many suicides among its adherents, presumably because it offered an accepted release from a life which was brutal and uncivilized. Yet official Greek and Roman attitudes to suicide were muted. Provided the Greek Senate was convinced that a case had been made, the individual who wished to commit suicide was allowed to do so by drinking hemlock. In Rome, suicide was never a penal offence except when it was committed by soldier, slave, or by one accused of a crime—clearly sanctions of expediency.

Centuries later there developed a very different attitude in which suicide was fiercely condemned and became equated with sin. This began when St. Augustine (A.D. 354–430) pronounced it a 'greater sin than any one might avoid by committing it'. There were no extenuating circumstances because it violates the sixth commandment, usurps the function of State and Church and avoids suffering which is divinely ordained.

There followed a repressive attitude to suicide, one which has lasted up until the present century. Its origins were undoubtedly complex. Although St. Augustine may have been prompted by the predilection of early Christians to choose voluntary martyrdom tantamount to suicide, there had always been an element of fear in man's reaction to deliberate self-destruction, and this antedated Christianity. It concerned what would happen to the suicide after his death and the repercussions which it might have for those who survived. According to orthodox Medieval Christianity the soul of a suicide is condemned to an eternity of hell. Dante (1265–1321) described their souls in his *Divine Comedy* as being encased in thorny withered trees on which the Harpies fed, inflicting wounds from which issued cries of lamentation and pain. In the Middle

Ages three penalties were imposed following a suicide. The first was degredation of the corpse by dragging it through the streets head down on a hurdle, which was followed by burial in non-consecrated ground. This was often at a crossroads with a stake driven through the heart and a stone over the face. Such a practice continued in London until 1823. The aim was to pin down the body so that the spirit would not return to harm or haunt the living. Forfeiture of goods was imposed in many European countires and this persisted until well into the nineteenth century.

The fact that some suicides are committed in a highly abnormal state of mind seems to have been recognized even in the earliest historical documents: Jews of Antiquity did not impose sanctions because they recognized suicide as necessarily an insane act. In the Middle Ages the insane suicide was excluded from religious and secular penal sanctions.

In spite of the ferocious medieval reaction against suicide the Renaissance of the sixteenth century produced its apologists who attempted to redress the balance. Erasmus (1466–1536) in *The Praise of Folly* (*Moriae Encomium*, 1509) which was a condemnation of church abuses, Sir Thomas More (1478–1535) in *Utopia* (1516), and Montaigne (1533–1592) in his *Essais*, all justified suicide under strictly defined circumstances, though they were careful to extol both sides of the argument.

In the seventeenth century attempts to understand suicide gathered momentum. John Donne (1572–1631) who as a clergyman acted with considerable courage of conviction asserted in his posthumous book *Biothanatos* (1644), the first defence of suicide in England, that God's power and mercy were great enough to remit the sin of suicide. Robert Burton (1577–1640) in *Anatomy of Melancholy* (1621) condemned suicide as being impious and abominable, stemming from a false pagan position; yet he pleaded a charitable attitude towards it and asserted that God could judge the matter. John Sym (1581–1637), also an English clergyman, identified those suicides who were sick in mind and who unlike the remainder would not suffer eternal damnation. Sym's *Life's Preservative against Self Killing* (1637) was the first English textbook on suicide, one which showed a concern for understanding and prevention. Those at risk were advised to avoid solitude, darkness, going over bridges or near the edge of steep places, and to be careful in using weapons such as knives. Premonitary signs were also listed, including abnormal behaviour, talking to the self and '. . . the speeches and actions of such persons immediately before the fact: which are some words threatening or foretelling something that may import so much; as that his friends shall not have him along to trouble them; or he will very shortly be rid out of all these troubles'.

Whilst attitudes of understanding and helping those at risk of suicide gathered momentum in the eighteenth century, a notable example being the essay *Of Suicide* in 1777 by David Hume (1711–1776), we also find evidence of fear and apprehension towards it, similar to that which we have noted throughout the whole of this historical review. There was widespread concern that suicide might increase in incidence and reach epidemic proportions. Many rumoured that it had already done so though there is no reliable evidence that such was the case. Suicide was associated particularly with the English and became known as 'the spleen' or 'the English malady', which was regarded as a disease in a land whose inhabitants showed a characteristic gloominess of temperament. George Cheyne (1671–1743) seems to have accepted this view and was challenged by its derisory nature into publishing in 1773 his book *The English Malady*, which he considered to be a new kind of disorder 'never afflicting such numbers in any known country'. He invoked inclement weather, rich heavy food, wealth, and sedentary living in great populous towns as causative factors. The Romantic Movement's glorification of death and Goethe's (1749–1832) *The Sorrow of Young Werther* probably accentuated fears that suicide would become greatly increased in incidence through fashion and imitation.

Our present-day understanding of suicide appears to have polarized into two divergent approaches, arising out of development of thought in the nineteenth century when sociologists such as Emil Durkheim (1858–1917) emphasized the importance of environment, yet at the same time the concept of mental illness as a disease with neuropathological correlates became elaborated. On the one hand, we have the statisticosocial search for causative situational factors and, on the other, a medicopsychiatric concern with factors in the individual, particularly the role of mental illness. These two approaches have become peculiarly difficult to equate. Each has its particular adherents who see the other view as less important, even irrelevant. The sociologist is inclined to regard the explanation of suicide in terms of mental illness as one which unjustifiably puts the blame on the person who commits it, eases the conscience of relatives, and hinders the search for situational causes, whilst the psychiatrist tends to the view that only intensive study of intrapsychic factors in the individual is relevant. Reconciliation between these two approaches remains one of the biggest challenges in our present-day attempts to understand and prevent suicide.

2

SUICIDE STATISTICS

Although suicide statistics have been documented by a large number of countries for many years, it is only comparatively recently that they have been critically evaluated in any systematic way. It is still far from clear exactly how dependable they are and how much we should infer from them. Perhaps their most vigorous critic has been Douglas (1967) who has contended that not only are suicide statistics so inaccurate as to be useless but also that they are rendered invalid as a result of gross variation in the way suicide is defined. He suggests that they permit no conclusions about national, district, and social differences in suicide. In contrast, Sainsbury (1973) has made a spirited defence of official suicide figures as follows:

> Suicide statistics have a privileged status among mortality figures because they are more extensive in scope and in detail than those available on any other deviant form of behaviour: in England, for instance, records cover more than 150 years. Consequently the rates of different social and demographic groups may be compared, trends studied and the ecology of suicide explored.

Before we look at the statistics themselves, we must examine the bases for these conflicting opinions.

2.1 A Critical Evaluation of Suicide Statistics

Validity and Reliability

The first question which must be asked is whether official figures achieve what they set out to do, i.e. to measure suicide and not to confuse it with death from other causes. In other words, what definition of suicide is used and how efficiently is it applied?

A review of attempts to formulate an adequate definition of suicide does not inspire us with confidence. At first glance the matter seems unequivocal and the World Health Organisation definition straight forward: the term 'suicidal act' denotes the self-infliction of injury with varying degrees of lethal intent and awareness of motive. Suicide means a suicidal act with fatal outcome (World Health Organisation, 1968b.) In some instances the evidence is overwhelming and the matter beyond doubt. Not infrequently, however, it can be very difficult to decide whether a death was suicidal, or accidental and unintentioned. Investigation is necessarily limited by the fact that it is retrospective, and the complexity of the psychodynamics involved makes ascertainment of intention hazardous. Even the most determined suicides may show evidence of ambivalence towards the matter in the weeks preceding their death. The situation is further complicated by the fact that self-destructive inclinations can be found in a wide variety of behaviour, e.g. car accidents or alcohol abuse, and these may not been seen primarily as suicidal (Menninger, 1938). How wide therefore should the definition be?

In spite of these difficulties, any attempt to study suicide has to face the need for a valid and reliable definition, and should accept that the fundamental aim must be to demonstrate a deliberate conscious action, undertaken by a person with the intention of ending his own life (Kastenbaum, 1976). Recent work has focused on the problem of measuring intent. Beck and others (Beck, Beck, and Kovacs, 1975; Beck, Resnik, and Lettieri, 1974; Beck, Schuyler, and Herman, 1974; Beck et al., 1976) have defined suicide as a wilful, self-inflicted life-threatening act which has resulted in death. This includes all situations in which the circumstances surrounding the deceased lead to the conclusion that the individual took a positive action with the primary purpose of ending his life. Intent is a complex phenomenon and its assessment, which is essentially inferential, needs to take into account evidence concerning the individual's mental state as well as the circumstances involved.

When we look at official suicide statistics the problem of definition is more complicated still. Although in some Scandinavian countries the categorization is a medical matter, in others, including the United Kingdom and the United States, the final decision is made by coroners whose training is often though not invariably mainly legal in nature, and the criteria of evidence are frequently those of the criminal court. If no objective evidence of proof of intent is available, e.g. by leaving a note or an overt declaration of intent made to an informant, then an open verdict is given. In other countries the critieria whereby intention is inferred are not clear and for all we know may be biased in a systematic way, perhaps embodying false assumptions about high-risk individual and social causes which inevitably increase the chance that a death in these groups may be categorized a suicide.

To be efficient statistics must not only involve correct categorization based on appropriate definition, but there must also be adequate case detection: we need to know the extent to which cases may be concealed and not reported, how thorough the examination of evidence has been, and to what extent suicides may be missed because of the undoubted tendency to avoid a diagnosis of suicide if doubt exists.

There is a great deal of evidence to suggest that official estimates of suicide lead to a considerable underestimate of its true incidence. McCarthy and Walsh (1975) estimated that in Dublin city and county during the years 1964–1968 the rate of suicide ascertained by psychiatrists' evaluation of medical records was four times greater than that estimated by official coroner's statistics. This problem has also been highlighted by work from the Los Angeles Suicide Prevention Center, where it has been shown that an intensive retrospective evaluation of the total situation surrounding deaths from uncertain causes, including interviews with relatives, may reveal more suicides than those declared through official statistics (Litman *et al.*, 1963).

For the purpose of compiling national statistics, suicides are taken as those deaths which have been categorized as such by coroners. When there is doubt about the intention of the deceased then either an accidental or open verdict is recorded by the coroner, and in compiling national figures these are assigned either to the accidental or undetermined groups of the International Classification of Disease. It has been shown that considerable differences exist between individual coroners in the proportion of open verdicts which they record (Barraclough, 1970), and this reflects on the nature of the undetermined categories in national statistics. Further, the accuracy of the collection and recording of data by coroners' officers has never been subjected to systematic enquiry (Holding and Barraclough, 1975; Barraclough, 1978b). If open verdicts, and hence 'undetermined' deaths, are mainly concealed suicides, the official statistics of suicide rates could be 22 per cent. too low. The high proportion of mental illness which these authors found in the 'undetermined' categories rises suspicion that such a proposition should be taken seriously. More recently, Adelstein and Mardon (1975) have attempted to arrive at a more broadly defined estimate of suicides by including 'undetermined' (E 980–989 ECD) and 'accidental poisoning' (ICD E 850–877) deaths, which has led to an increase of 50 per cent. over official suicide rates for 1974 in England and Wales (see Table 2, p. 18).

In face of these many difficulties, Sainsbury (1973) has presented a considerable body of evidence to suggest that suicide statistics can still be of major value in the study of suicide provided they are used appropriately and their deficiencies are taken fully into account. Thus in each of fourteen countries there was found to be an extremely high degree of consistency (with a correlation of 0.95) in suicide rates over a ten-year period (Sainsbury and Barraclough, 1968). Again, in twenty-five countries the rankings for suicide rates were not significantly altered when 'undetermined' deaths were combined with suicides, suggesting that national inconsistencies in defining suicide were probably not important (Barraclough, 1973).

The intrinsic value of coroners' verdicts has also been underlined by a study which included all the coroners' districts in England and Wales. Suicide rates for the two years 1950 and 1960 were found to be reasonably stable, and this held even when there had been a change of coroner (Barraclough, 1970; Sainsbury and Barraclough, 1968). Further, the pattern of suicide rates throughout the various London boroughs appears to be related to social factors pertaining in each, whether one or several coroners are involved; this suggests that categorization of suicides is not a random process but one which bears a consistent and systematic relationship to social factors. Affirmation of the reliability of official statistics has also come recently from Helsinki (Lönnqvist, 1977), where an intensive retrospective study, involving scrutiny of inquest and medical records, as well as death certificate data of all accidental deaths, suicides, homicides, and undetermined deaths, has shown that suicide statistics probably underestimated suicide by at the most 9 per cent. in 1970–1971.

The continuing debate concerning the value of official statistics on suicide means that we must never accept them at face value, and extrapolations from them should always be scrutinized in terms of their validity and reliability. Raw figures are, of course, of little value and it is usual to calculate the suicide rate for the population or community in question. Thus the suicide rate for any population is defined as the number of suicides occurring in persons over the age of 15 during the course of one year. The populations under investigation of course vary: we may refer to rates in males or females, either in terms of the total nation or as subnational divisions such as regions, towns, or even suburban districts. Whilst the calculation of rates helps to standardize data and so permit comparison over time or between groups, it is important to recognize that this technique may itself lead to erroneous interpretation. Calculation of the population at risk can be very unreliable, especially when based on census data which may well be inaccurate, perhaps through being out of date or because of high population mobility, as in certain urban areas. Younger age groups tend to be underreported to a national census as are non-whites in the United States. When the population is small great care should be exercised in calculating suicide rates because relatively minor errors of enumeration in the base population can lead to large differences in rates. When the numbers of cases are small, as for the younger age groups, then relatively great changes in rates can occur due to random fluctuation of a comparatively rare event (Linden and Breed, 1976).

2.2 Uses of Suicide Statistics

International comparisons of suicide rates have long been popular though their interpretation is hazardous in view of inevitable variation in methods of diagnosis and case detection from one country to another; it is generally accepted that intranational analysis is more reliable and amenable to detailed analysis. Trends in national rates allow us to monitor changes in any given country over an extended period of time. Intranational comparison may involve different areas of the country or various population subgroups according to such criteria as age, sex, ethnic group, and marital status or clinical variables such as the presence of physical and mental illness.

Sainsbury (1973) has stated clearly and succinctly how suicide statistics may be used in the search for causes:

> For all practical epidemiological purposes, underreporting or seeking the elusive 'absolute' rate of suicide is of small consequence. What matters, and what the epidemiologist needs to establish clearly, is whether the differences he observes between the rates of particular social, clinical or other categories are valid: we discern causes by showing that certain groups of people differ in having an exceptional incidence of suicide.

A word or caution is, however, still required. Even when a consistent association is found between social conditions and the incidence of suicide, it is necessary to remember that the relationship may be indirect and not necessarily causal. Such associations may, however, provide useful leads to other related variables such as mental disorder which might not themselves be measured easily. When dealing with small population subgroups such as ethnic minorities it has already been pointed out that calculation of rates may be highly unreliable if small numbers are involved.

International comparisons

About 52 nations out of a total of 125 report their suicide rate to the World Health Organisation. Table 1 illustrates suicide rates for 21 nations reporting to the W.H.O. in this way during the periods 1952–1954 and 1961–1963.

Marked international differences in suicide rates clearly do occur and the rate in each country shows a considerable degree of stability and consistency over a period of time. These figures are of little use, and are even misleading, if they are abused by making them the basis for unjustified conjecture. On the other hand, they should at this stage in our knowledge at least facilitate the study of variations in definition and detection of suicide as well as in the compilation of national statistics, between the various countries involved.

TABLE 1   National death rates from suicide 1952–1954 and 1961–1963 (nations reporting statistics to W.H.O.)

	Suicide rates per 100,000	
	1952–1954	1961–1963
Hungary	33.9	—
Denmark	31.9	24.2
Japan	31.4	24.7
Austria	29.9	28.3
Switzerland	28.8	23.3
Czechoslovakia	28.2	—
Finland	25.8	29.0
Germany (Federal Republic)	23.6	24.1
Sweden	23.4	21.7
France	20.3	20.7
Australia	14.9	19.6
United States	14.1	15.6
England and Wales	13.8	15.1
New Zealand	13.5	13.0
Poland	12.8	—
Israel	10.1	—
Norway	9.8	10.0
Canada	9.5	11.1
Netherlands	9.0	9.1
Italy	6.4	7.1
Scotland	7.5	11.4

Source: World Health Organization, 1968a, 1968b.

14

Age and sex

Both in England and Wales and in the United States, suicide accounts for about 1 per cent. of all deaths. Its incidence increases with age, and national statistics reveal it to be more common in males than in females. The average suicide rates according to age groups in Bristol during the period 1968–1973 are shown in Figure 1. In England and Wales the 1974 suicide rate for the total population was 79 per million, the male rate (95 per million) exceeding that of females (64 per million) by 50 per cent. (Adelstein and Mardon, 1975). Although suicide is numerically greater in older people it is the fourth most common cause of death in young adults aged 15 to 34 years. In the United States during the period 1969–1971 the rates were 178 and 71 per million in white males and females respectively (Linden and Breed, 1976). Suicide is extremely rare in children under 10 years of age; in England and Wales it occurred during

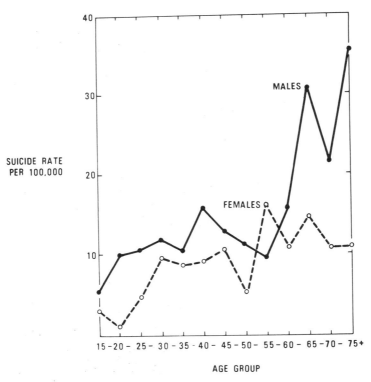

FIGURE 1. Suicide Bristol 1968–73. (Average annual age specific rates—Coroner's statistics)

the period 1962–1968 in 10 to 14 year olds at a rate of one child out of every 800,000. Suicide accounts for only 0.6 per cent. of all deaths in that age group (Shaffer, 1974).

National trends

It is seen from Figure 2 that in England and Wales during the period 1901–1970 there was a general tendency for older male suicides to decrease in numbers. In contrast, rates in females tended to rise. A significant proportion of the twenty-three countries in which suicide statistics have been kept since 1920 also show this increase in female suicide rates, and again it is the older age groups that have been mainly affected. In England and Wales young adults of both sexes up to 25 years of age showed a tendency for the incidence of suicide to rise during the period 1955–1965 and in the case of young men this was also found in a significant proportion of other nations (Sainsbury, 1973).

Close examination of Figure 2 reveals that in the late 1960s there was a substantial fall in suicide rates in all ages except the youngest. More recent trends have been analysed by Adelstein and Mardon (1975) and it is clear that the official total male suicide rate which has been falling since 1973 was lower in 1974 (at 95 per million) than at any time in this century in England and Wales. In contrast the female official suicide rate in 1974 (at 64 per million) was 33 per cent. higher than in 1901.

Examination of age-specific suicide rates reveals that the greatest improvement in recent years has occurred in males over 45 years of age, whilst a steady rise has occurred in the 25 to 34 year old males since 1970. In females during the early 1970s, there has also been a fall in the rates for those of 45 years or older (with a slight turnup in 1973–1974), but rates in females aged 34 to 44 years rose sharply. A progressive and steady rise has also occurred in females aged 15 to 24 years.

The overall effect of these trends has been to reduce the differences between the various groups involved. In 1961, elderly males and females committed suicide seven and eight times more commonly than did young adults of the same sex, whereas these factors were three and four respectively in 1974. The effect has also been to reduce the preponderance of male suicide: in the period 1901–1905 three men to every woman committed suicide whereas in 1974 the ratio was three to two in the United Kingdom (Adelstein and Mardon, 1975).

In the United States similar trends have occurred in suicide rates in recent decades, the reduction in rates for older males being the most marked. Rates in young persons there have increased for both males and

16

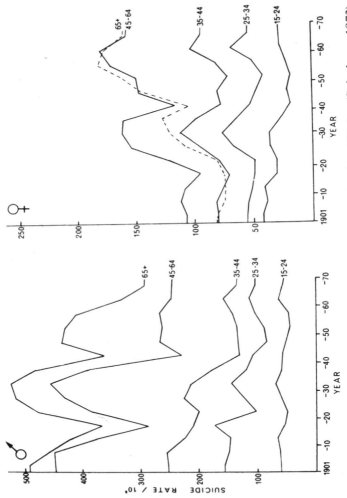

FIGURE 2. Suicide rates 1901–70 by sex and age : England and Wales. (Sainsbury, 1973)

females during the period 1950–1970, with white males still outnumbering white females by more than two to one (Linden and Breed, 1976).

Urban/rural living

Statistics have long suggested that suicide rates in rural areas are less than in towns and cities. Figures for England and Wales in the period 1959–1963 suggested a downward gradient from conurbations, through large, medium, and small urban areas to rural conditions. By the period 1970–1972 a steep fall had occurred in the rate of conurbation suicide, less so far smaller urban areas. Rates in rural areas had also decreased, but to a smaller extent. The end result has been that rural suicide rates for males in 1970 exceeded those in medium and small urban areas (Adelstein and Mardon, 1975). It does appear that differences in suicide rates between rural and urban living are beginning to break down and it is unwise to read too much into them. We would need to be reassured in particular that case detection and scrutiny of evidence in rural conditions is as efficient as in towns and cities, and at present we know little about such possible sources of unreliability.

Marital status

A consistent relationship has been found between marital status and rates for suicide, which are increased in divorcees, widows and widowers, and the single (never married), with a decreasing gradient in that order. Widows and widowers appeared to be at particularly high risk in many age groups. Suicide mortality is lowest in those who are married at the time of death (Registrar General, 1967).

Season

Suicide has its highest incidence during April, May, and June in the fifteen Northern Hemisphere countries that record and report their monthly statistics. In Australia a similiar rise in incidence occurs during the months of spring to mid summer. Males appear to be more likely than females to such seasonal variation in suicide rates (World Health Organisation, 1961).

Social class

Our Bristol survey suggests that interpretation of the social class distribution of suicide in the light of National Census data must be

ertaken with caution. In those central parts of the city which have
‚h suicide rates, 21.8 per cent. of residents could not be allocated to a
socioeconomic group according to the 1971 Census.

Using the conventional classification based on occupation and
employment status the incidence of suicide in England and Wales in
recent years (Table 2) has been greatest in class V (unskilled workers).
Class I (professional) and IV (partly skilled) show smaller increases above
the national average, but in classes II and III (lower professionals and
executives and the skilled manual and non-manual workers) rates are
below the expected level.

For social class I the excess of suicides is found in those over 35 years of
age, with the younger age groups showing fewer than expected suicides.
In classes IV and V, on the other hand, the observed deaths exceed those
expected at all ages, but this is especially marked for individuals under 35
years of age. Dublin (1963) has pointed out that the suicide rate is
increased in groups at the two extremes of the economic scale in the
United States as well as in England and Wales. Weiss (1954) found the
highest suicide rates in the upper social classes in New Haven,
Connecticut.

Sainsbury (1975) has pointed out that social class analysis of this kind
does not bring out the fact that high suicide risk is not necessarily closely
related to social and economic status. Occupation mortality tables show
that besides the professionals (especially physicians, amongst whom
psychiatrists show the highest rates), other groups such as hotel-keepers
and bookmakers are in the top range of suicide risk. Occupations with the

TABLE 2   Deaths in England and Wales officially classified as suicide, accidental
poisoning, and open verdicts and SMRs for males aged 15–64, 1970–1972,
analysed by social class

Social class	Suicide		Accidental poisoning		Open verdicts		'Estimated suicides'	
	Observed deaths	SMR	Observed deaths	SMR	Observed deaths	SMR	Observed deaths	SMR
I	274	110	44	105	48	77	366	104
II	819	90	145	95	162	70	1,126	87
III	2,039	85	316	76	471	77	2,826	83
IV	993	117	163	112	264	122	1,420	118
V	685	184	139	214	222	231	1,046	196

Source: Adelstein and Mardon, 1975.

lowest rates range from clergymen to coal miners. He postulates that degree of integration or isolation in a community that membership of a occupational group entails is just as important as the status it implies. This would also account for the fact that indigenous poverty does not bear a close relation to suicidal risk.

Ethnic and religious grouping

When dealing with population subgroups problems of enumeration by means of census data can become difficult, especially when the populations are small in size and racial categorization is ambiguous. The most comprehensive statistics on ethnic grouping concern the non-white American population. Evidence has long been cited to suggest that black Americans have lower suicide rates than whites. Further, there is evidence to suggest that young non-white individuals are particularly liable to underenumeration by national census, and hence their suicide rates might have been overestimated. It is likely, however, that suicide rates have increased in the non-white American population of all ages during the last thirty years; in some north-eastern states the suicide rates in young blacks may now be the same as in young whites. The older black population probably still has a lower suicide rate than that of whites (Linden and Breed, 1976).

The early work of Durkheim in Europe concluded that Protestant populations consistently showed higher rates of suicide than did Catholics or Jews, and many inferences have been drawn with regard to the significance of these findings. Shneidman (1976) points out, however, that at other times and places these findings have been reversed, and presumably the relationship between religious persuasion and suicide risk is a complex one: many other factors contribute to the suicide rate in population subgroups varying with time and situation.

2.3 Method of Suicide

Since 1962, in England and Wales a remarkable drop has occurred in the number of suicides due to domestic coal gas poisoning, this being undoubtedly related to a reduction in the carbon monoxide content of town gas, which occurred about 1963, and more recently to the conversion to natural gas (Figure 3). An increase has occurred in suicides due to poisoning, particularly with antidepressants, hypnotics and sedatives (other than barbiturates), tranquillizers, and salicylates. This has offset a fall in suicides due to barbiturate poisoning, although in 1973

20

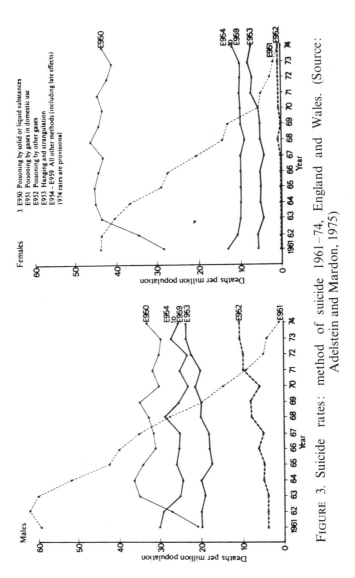

FIGURE 3. Suicide rates: method of suicide 1961–74, England and Wales. (Source: Adelstein and Mardon, 1975)

it still contributed to 27 per cent. of all suicide deaths in England and Wales. Drug overdosage has become the most common method of suicide in both sexes, accounting for 67 and 35 per cent. of suicides in females and males respectively. Hanging and strangling are frequently used by males, but far less commonly by females. In the United States shooting is more frequent, accounting in 1964 for about 56 per cent. of white male and 25 per cent. of white female suicides. Compared with England and Wales, suicide by poisoning in the United States is far less common in males, though it appears to be just as common in females, especially in the black population (Swanson and Breed, 1976).

3

CORRELATES AND CAUSES OF SUICIDE

In our search for causes of suicide we encounter many problems. Each suicide is in many ways a unique event relevant only to the individual concerned and his own life situation. It follows that we cannot assume that findings from a limited number of cases are necessarily applicable to suicides in general; conversely, in trying to understand the individual suicide it can be very misleading to invoke, without adequate discrimination, data based on suicide statistics and large-scale population surveys. Bearing these points in mind, we first need to discuss personal and situational concomitants of suicide, those factors which by the regularity of their association may have some implication in its cause.

3.1 Personal Factors

Age and sex

These have already been discussed in the previous chapter on the statistics of suicide. At all ages suicide rates in males exceed those in females, increasing sharply with age. The trend in very recent years has been for the rates in older persons to fall though some younger adult groups in both sexes have tended to show a consistent rise since the early 1970s. It is not fruitful to add conjecture to these statistics at this stage, but we need to keep them in mind in the ensuing discussion of suicide concomitants.

Previous history of mental disorder

Studies in several countries have revealed a consistent picture of increased suicide rates in persons who have either been under psychiatric care at some time previously or were acutally receiving such care at the time they

22

killed themselves (World Health Organisation, 1968b). This appears to be the case whether the reports were concerned with mental hospital or outpatient populations, or those detected through community case registers. In Massachusetts, residents who had been in mental hospitals had a suicide rate thrity-six times that of the general population (Temoche, Pugh, and MacMohan, 1964). The incidence of previous psychiatric contact in suicides has been estimated to be as high as between 33 and 50 per cent. (Barraclough *et al.*, 1974; Seager and Flood, 1965).

Psychological disturbance at the time of suicide

Those studies which have been based on coroners' records have estimated that about two-thirds of suicide deaths are related to mental illness (World Health Organization, 1968b). When more detailed investigation has been undertaken, however, the proportion judged to be mentally ill has risen considerably: two major studies of this kind deserve particular mention. Robins *et al.* (1959) interviewed close friends and relatives and other associates of 134 suicides detected by coroners' data in St. Louis and St. Louis county: 94 per cent. of the suicides were judged to have been mentally ill with clear evidence of a recognizable type of psychiatric disorder. The interviews were systematic and extensive, lasting about two hours and ranging over a wide variety of information concerning past and present symptoms, social history, and circumstances surrounding the event. In a later English study Barraclough *et al.* (1974) interviewed key informants of 100 consecutive suicides defined by coroners' inquests on residents in the county of West Sussex and in Portsmouth. Systematic and thorough interviews were again used and standardization was achieved by joint scrutiny of the data. Other documents such as hospital notes were used in corroboration. A controlled, matched population sample was also interviewed. Of the suicides, 93 per cent. were diagnosed retrospectively as having been mentally ill at the time they died.

These studies, though detailed, were concerned only with small numbers of patients and they might not have provided a fully comprehensive picture of suicides in general. They are also open to the criticism that the way in which key informants reconstructed events may have been biased, and the investigators themselves were of course aware of the fact that suicide had occurred. The use of standardized interviews and comparison with a control sample goes some way to answering this kind of criticism and we are bound to concede that major recognisable distress probably precedes the act of suicide in many cases. This receives strong support from the additional finding that many suicides seek help in

24

the weeks immediately preceding their deaths. Robins and his coworkers estimated that 25 to 53 per cent. of the suicides which they studied had received medical or psychiatric care in the preceding months: the more recent English study found that 66 per cent. had done so compared with 25 per cent. in the control group (40 per cent. in the last week compared with 7 per cent. in controls).

Mental disorders associated with high suicide risk

Review of the inquest and medical records of suicides has revealed that certain mental illnesses have a particularly high association with suicide risk: by far the most common of these are depressive illness and alcohol dependence.

Although there is much debate with regard to the cause of *depressive illness*, particularly whether it is reactive to some environmental factor as opposed to intrinsic or endogenous causes due to some genetically determined physicochemical disorder, its cardinal symptoms are quite clear. These include insomnia, weight loss, anorexia, depressed appearance, complaint of depressed mood, loss of interest and concentration, apathy, delusional ideas of guilt, hypochondriasis, and pessimism about the future. Such symptoms are generally regarded as an indication that depressive illness is present. It is precisely this state of mind which is so commonly associated with suicide. The evidence for this association has been sought in two ways: first, by determining how many depressives kill themselves, and second, by assessing the proportion of suicides who were depressed at the time of their death. Of those persons who have at some time suffered a severe depressive illness, between 11 and 17 per cent. will eventually kill themselves (Fremming, 1951; Helgason, 1964; Pitts and Winokur, 1964), a much higher incidence than in any other mental disorder. About half of suicides show evidence of a depressive illness in the weeks preceding their death, the incidence being slightly greater in women than in men (Barraclough *et al.*, 1974; Capstick, 1960; Robins *et al.*, 1959; Sainsbury, 1955). Quite often there has been a previous history of depressive illness, a much greater incidence of previous attempts at suicide (46 per cent. compared with 6 per cent. in a controlled sample of persons with depressive illness who have not killed themselves), and a history of depressive illness in 20 per cent. of first-degree relatives (Barraclough *et al.*, 1974). Persons over 40 years of age with severe depressive illness are particularly vulnerable to suicide and this kind of illness is four times more likely to lead to suicide in men than in women (Murphy and Robins, 1967; Pitts and Winokur, 1964; Sainsbury, 1962). It has long been recognized that the stage of onset and recovery in depressive illness may be particularly associated with suicide risk: in one series of depressed suicides 30 per cent. died within a month of discharge from psychiatric hospital (Pokorny, 1964).

In looking for the reasons why depressive illness has such a striking relationship to suicide the central symptoms themselves are clearly relevant. Depression of mood accompanied by loss of ability to feel warmth towards others, loss of religious belief, perhaps delusional ideas of guilt and being ill, soon lead to a state of hopelessness and despair. The drive towards self-destruction in the severely depressed arises out of a mental state which negates the basic assumption of life. It represents such mental distress that death seems likely to be the only solution, irrespective of its implications for the self and others. The natural history of a severe depressive illness is frequently one of recurrent breakdowns, and this itself may increase the individual's sense of failure and hopelessness, particularly when many episodes of illness have occurred. In trying to explain the close relationship between severe depression and suicide we should not, however, confine ourselves merely to the inherent nature of the illness itself, but in addition we need to examine the way in which others respond to it. The detection of serious suicidal ideas can of course be difficult because of the patient's reticence which arises out of a conviction that intervention is irrelevant and useless. The depressive tends to remain undeclared and undetected: he does not impinge himself upon us through grossly disordered behaviour and, though he often seeks help, the full extent of his depression may still not be recognized. If multiple depressive episodes occur we tend to be less sympathetic and we become inclined to see the illness in terms of hysterical secondary gain. The patient is exhorted to think of the effect that he is having on others and his duty towards them, and he is urged to be less dependent upon people around him. The increased suicide risk in older depressives may be due as much to a sense of alienation and isolation generated by the inability of others to retain sympathy and understanding as any inherent worsening of the illness itself with increasing age.

Alcohol dependence is second only to depressive illness as a concomitant of suicide. When alcohol intake has reached such a degree that it causes problems then pathological dependence has developed. A person is said to be chronically addicted to alcohol when it interferes with his mental or physical health and there are inevitable major socioeconomic complications. Withdrawal symptoms of increased anxiety, tremor, or even hallucinations and delirium tremens may provide incontrovertible evidence that physical dependence has developed. Of chronic alcohol addicts who have received psychiatric treatment in hospital, between 7 and 20 per cent. have been found to have committed suicide during a five-year follow-up, an incidence which is 75 to 85 times greater than in the general population (Kessel and Grossman, 1961; Norvig and Nielsen, 1956). When a total population cohort is followed up, or case register data are used, the incidence of suicide in alcohol addicts is still much higher than in the general population (Gardner, Bahn, and Mack, 1964; Helgason, 1964). Samples of persons who have committed suicide show that between a quarter and a third of the men were addicted to alcohol at the time of death. The incidence of chronic alcohol addiction in female suicides is probably less, though it may be as much as 20 per cent. (World Health Organisation, 1968b). Post mortem assays of blood alcohol levels suggest that almost half of male and one-fifth of female suicides have taken significant amounts of alcohol within the previous few hours (James, 1966). Alcohol addict suicides often show the features of depressive illness; they tend to have been drinking for many years, having started in their early twenties, and to have significant physical complications. About two-thirds of them will have 'attempted suicide' previously, compared with 10 per cent. in alcoholics who have not completed suicide and who have been detected through general population surveys. Frequently the picture is of the older alcoholic who has lost a spouse through death or separation or who has an unhappy marital relationship.

Alcohol is, of course, a depressant of the central nervous system and its direct pharmacological effects undoubtedly may produce depression of mood. The close relationship between alcohol addiction and depressive illness reflects both this and the possibility that persons predisposed to depression may use alcohol in an attempt to relieve their distress. The reduction of inhibition and release of aggressive behaviour, both direct effects of alcohol itself, may produce the precipitating factor in someone who otherwise may not have the courage to undertake self-destruction. Hallucinatory and delirious withdrawal states themselves also increase the risk involved. As the illness proceeds, the alcoholic becomes increasingly isolated from help and sympathy. A process of progressive alienation, itself relevant to suicide risk and which has already been hypothesized in the case of depressive suicides, applies also to the alcoholic who kills himself, only more so.

Organic psychoses are also associated with high suicide risk. In the advanced stages there is loss of insight through severe intellectual deterioration and memory impairment, but initially there may be marked depression with suicidal ideas because the patient can appreciate what is happening to him.

Some reports suggest that 4 per cent. of suicides have *chronic organic brain syndromes* (Dorpat and Ripley, 1960; Robins *et al.*, 1959a). When epilepsy is complicated by depression there is a considerably increased risk of suicide, and the necessary access which an epileptic has to anticonvulsant drugs such as phenobarbitone which are lethal in overdose is of course a major problem. Dangerous situations also arise when complex behavioural difficulties bring the epileptic into conflict with others, particularly when there are doubts about the true extent of his disability. Five out of thirty temporal lobe epileptics who had experienced previous psychological difficulties and who underwent temporal lobectomy subsequently committed suicide (Taylor, 1972). Seven per cent. of epileptics who also exhibit organic brain syndromes with memory and intellectual impairment eventually kill themselves.

The incidence of suicide in *schizophrenia* is less clear, probably because of the considerable variation in the way this illness is conceptualized from one country to another. In North America, many patients who are diagnosed as schizophrenic would be regarded as depressives by European psychiatrists. It is therefore not very easy to interpret findings such as those of Osmond and Hoffer (1967) who found suicide rates in schizophrenia twenty times greater than those in the general population. The large cohort study in Iceland revealed a 2 per cent. expectation of suicide in schizophrenics, followed up until they were 60 years of age. Psychotic illnesses of this kind often cause major disorder of behaviour and can lead to recurrent spells of hospitalization. Not infrequently, some kind of defect state remains with regard to drive, initiative, and ability to relate normally to others. It is of interest therefore that at least one study (Shneidman, Farberow, and Leonard, 1962) has pointed out that the stage of apparent improvement and remission of florid schizophrenic symptoms is one of particular risk for suicide, presumably because the patient has regained some insight into his illness and is facing the prospect of trying to cope independently once again in the community. This is an interesting parallel with the high incidence of suicide in depressives soon after their discharge from hospital.

A proportion of the increased mortality due to *drug addiction*, especially that which involves injection techniques, is due to suicide; British male heroin addicts have a suicide rate which is more than fifty times greater than that in the general population (James, 1967).

Whilst the traditional stereotype of the older person with depressive illness and relatively stable life pattern has been emphasized in many studies, other point out that it is not typical of all suicides. Individuals with severe personality difficulties may constitute between a third and a half of all cases (McCulloch, Philip, and Carstairs, 1967; Ovenstone and Kreitman, 1974; Seager and Flood, 1965). In this group, which tends to be younger than other suicides, longstanding personality problems of a sociopathic kind lead to a chronic destruction of family life, a subculture of violence, alcohol, and drug abuse, and frequently one or more episodes of 'attempted suicide'. In fact, such suicides may be a reflection of the massive increase in 'attempted suicides' in recent years. Chronic situational stress becomes progressively more severe in these individuals and they commit suicide in the setting of recurrent quarrels, social disintegration, and severe alienation from those around them.

Physical illness

This occurs more often than expected in persons who kill themselves, particularly in older suicides (Dorpat and Ripley, 1960). It is usually associated with severe depressive symptoms and has been estimated to be a contributory factor in 29 per cent. of suicides, probably even more in the elderly (Sainsbury, 1962). Chronic life-threatening disease is particularly relevant to suicide risk when other factors such as serious depressive symptoms are present. Closely related is, of course, the way in which various drugs that are used in the treatment of physical illness may themselves increase the risk of suicide. This may occur not only because they can be misused by someone who is otherwise seriously depressed but also due to the fact that in certain vulnerable individuals their direct pharmacological action may precipitate serious depression. Perhaps the most striking example of this is reserpine, which was at one time used in the treatment of hypertension, but now the most commonly used drugs causing depression are long-acting depot phenothiazine preparations used in the treatment of schizophrenia, barbiturates, and contraceptives (Lancet, 1977; Whitlock and Evans, 1978). A wide variety of other drugs may also be relevant, depending on the predisposing factors in the individual patient, and should be suspected when depressive symptoms appear during their use.

Psychological mechanisms

The psychoanalytic school has seen suicide as an act of inwardly directed aggression. Freud's explanatory theory of melancholia suggested that loss of a love object leads to withdrawal of energy from it back into the self. A process of identification of the self with the lost object occurs, and where there had also been hostility towards it severe depression may develop, perhaps with suicidal risk.

Menninger (1938) emphasized the complexity of suicidal motivation and elaborated the role of primary impulses of destructiveness and creativeness. When the outward manifestation of these is thwarted in some way, they are turned back upon themselves. If the destructive force prevails, then there is the wish to kill and to be killed; sometimes a primary self-directed aggression, the wish to die, also plays a part. Menninger also explains various self-damaging behaviours such as alcoholism as a form of chronic suicide in which constructive forces partially neutralize those which are destructive. According to such theories, which emphasize the role of aggressive drive in leading to suicide, we would expect to find anger and resentment towards others intimately bound up with guilt and hostility towards the self in suicidal individuals.

Identification with a love object that has died can itself strengthen suicide motivation by introducing the concept of rejoining the loved person by killing the self. Attitudes towards death, particularly whether it is final or merely a stage towards some other better type of existence, must also be relevant.

Other theoretical approaches including those of Horney, Adler, and Sullivan, have been reviewed by Farberow (1957).

If we are to evaluate the thought processes of those who commit suicide, prospective studies are theoretically the most sound, but they are of course practically impossible to achieve: they would involve following up a large well-documented population for a very long period of time in order to pick up a sufficient number of suicides to permit comparison with the remainder. We are left with retrospective attempts at reconstruction and these are grossly limited both by inadequate information and potential bias in interpretation. The literature has recently been reviewed by Neuringer (1976). Sometimes attempts are made to circumvent this problem by studying individuals who have 'attempted suicide' and survived, but these do not necessarily represent true suicides. Neuringer (1961) confined his studies to persons who had survived serious attempts, and demonstrated a form of dichotomous thinking in which issues are conceptualized in a polarized way, resulting in a tendency to choose extremes in various attitude scales. He further (1964) showed that they were more rigid and inflexible in their responses when compared with patients who had psychosomatic and medical problems. In spite of the methodological limitations, these studies suggest that we should look further at the way styles of thinking, with obvious implications for problem solving, resilience, and adaptability to life situations, may contribute to the sequence of thought processes which can lead to suicide.

The use of suicide notes in the study of suicide ideation has also been reviewed recently (Shneidman, 1976; Tripodes, 1976). They tend to show dichotomous logic and can be distinguished from false notes by the fact that they show more evidence of hostility, self-blame, and greater use of very specific names and instructions to the survivors.

Previous personality

The enduring qualities of an individual's psychological makeup we call personality, and its evaluation must necessarily be based upon patterns of behaviour, thoughts, and feelings over an extended period of time. Predisposition to suicide through personality structure is again difficult to investigate. Evaluation of hospital case notes have suggested that psychiatric patients who kill themselves are often more aggressive, demanding, dependent, and dissatisfied than others (Farberow, Shneidman, and Neuringer, 1966; Flood and Seager, 1968), though such difficult behaviour might to some extent reflect recently developed mental illness or justifiable frustration concerning their situation rather than longstanding traits of personality. Evidence from medical notes does not reveal any striking relationship between type of previous personality and suicide, though this is not perhaps surprising in view of the difficulties in categorizing personality and inadequacy of available data. However, in the Bristol study of Flood and Seager (1968) only 4 per cent. were regarded as having had a normal previous personality compared with 23 per cent. of matched control patients. Shaffer's (1974) study of thirty suicides in children under 15 years of age is notable for the detailed information which was obtained with regard to previous personality patterns. Categories which appeared consistently in data from records and interviews with teachers included attitudes of 'chip on shoulder', impulsive and erratic behaviour with poor self-control, a tendency to be quiet and uncommunicative, or perfectionist and self-critical.

Family and childhood

In the absence of adequate prospective studies it is not surprising that relatively little is known about the childhood of suicides. In the rare instances where suicide occurs in childhood the family situation is more immediate and information is therefore easier to obtain. Shaffer (1974) found that about a quarter of his series of child suicides were from broken homes, a further 20 per cent. of the parents separating and divorcing four years after the child's death. Similar findings have been foun adolescent suicides (Micic, Rajs, and Pandurovic, 1967; Tuckman, Youngman, and Leifer, 1966); we cannot generalize from these figures to suicides in general, which usually occur much later in life and therefore may have a less direct relationship to early family experiences. Evidence with regard to this is conflicting, and negative findings may merely reflect the methodological problems involved (Bunch et al., 1971a, 1971b; Lester, 1972).

In view of the increasing body of evidence that childhood bereavement may predispose to depression many years later (Birtchnell, 1970a, 1970b) this area of research needs clarification. A history of family disruption in childhood seems to be common in the important group of suicides emphasized by workers in Edinburgh (McCulloch, Philip, and Carstairs, 1967; Ovenstone and Kreitman, 1974) consisting of younger sociopathic patients who have a history of previous attempted suicide.

3.2   Situational Factors

An individual's life situation has obvious relevance to suicide and it has been investigated in two ways. The first, which is an ecological approach, examines the distribution of suicide throughout a community and the way in which it varies with social and other environmental factors within it. Such an approach has to depend upon census data and relatively crude indirect indices of life situations, but they provide a useful bird's-eye view of the total problem. The second way is to examine the social situation of suicides themselves through retrospective review of available infor- mation; this is, of course, a more direct approach and is the only way to validate findings from an ecological study.

The social aspects of suicide were first studied systematically in the nineteenth century by Durkheim (1951) who claimed that an individual's life situation, particularly his relationship with others in the community, is the paramount factor relevant to suicide risk. Loss of integration with the group, loss of controls imposed upon him, whether they be of religious, family, or of wider social origin, lead to a sense of isolation and morbid individualism thereby predisposing to 'egotistic' suicide. Closely related to this is the concept of 'anomic' suicide in which the individual's aspirations and desires are at variance with and cannot be met by society; this is particularly liable to occur at times of massive social changes. 'Altruistic' suicide is related to massive group authority over the individual, whereby he may choose his own death if it is for the good of the whole. A good example would be Titus Oates of the Scott Antarctic Expedition; suffering from severe frostbite he found it increasingly difficult to keep up with the others in their attempt to return to base. Eventually he went out into the blizzard saying 'I am just going outside and may be some time'. Presumably he believed that in sacrificing himself he was increasing the chances that the others might have to survive.

Although we may feel that Durkheim overemphasized social factors in suicide at the expense of those which are individual and psychological, his work has been the stimulus for much consequent research into the social aspects of suicide. Cavan (1928) took up the ecological approach and demonstrated that suicide was not uniformly distributed in Chicago in the period 1919–1921, but was concentrated in four communities near the central business area characterized by shifting populations, cheap hotels and rooming houses, and an impersonal, lonely disillusioned type of existence. Studies in other cities produced similar results (Faris 1948, Mowrer, 1942; Schmid, 1937).

Sainsbury's (1955) investigation of the ecology of suicide in London was also inspired by the earlier work of Durkheim and began with the hypothesis that social mobility and social isolation are important concomitants of suicide because of the resulting instability and lack of order and purpose in community life. His findings are striking. During a 25-year period (1919–1945) significant and consistent differences in suicide rates were found amongst the various London Boroughs in spite of considerable changes in their populations. Rates correlated highly with indices of social isolation (persons living alone and in boarding houses), social mobility, proportion of immigrants, and social disorganization (divorce, illegitimacy). No increased risk was found to be associated with overcrowding or poverty. The individual social characteristics of a series of suicides were then examined from coroners' data and in a third of these external social stress was thought to be important as a cause of the suicide itself: 27.4 per cent. were living alone, far more often than persons in the general population, and the records suggested that loneliness was an important adverse factor accounting for differential suicide rates in the boroughs and subdistrict. Its high incidence in groups such as the aged, unemployed, divorced, and immigrants appeared to be in some degree explicable in terms of social isolation. Of interest is the fact that the records suggested that unemployment or loss of employment was also important, though the ecological study did not show this. Life situational concomitants of suicide consistent with Durkheim's original hypothesis were thus vividly demonstrated by Sainsbury's study. They were found by Whitlock (1973a, 1973b) still to apply in London during the period 1959–1963. In large cities suicide is particularly high in central areas where the relevant socioeconomic conditions tend to dominate other environmental factors (Cavan, 1928; Lönnqvist, 1977; Sainsbury, 1955; Schmid 1928). Bristol is no exception to this pattern (Figure 4): its social ecology is described later (Chapter 9) when the distribution of non fatal self harm in the city is discussed in detail.

It is likely that since the early 1960s a relatively new social stereotype of suicide has gradually increased in importance and one which in many ways is different from the long-accepted picture of the elderly, socially isolated and depressed. It concerns younger persons living in over-crowded conditions and who exhibit longstanding disturbed behaviour

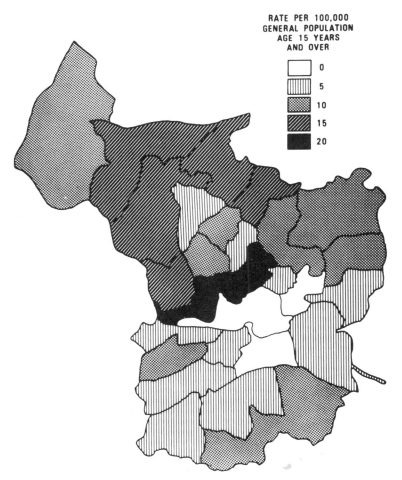

FIGURE 4. Bristol City electoral wards suicide rates 1968–73

which has brought them into conflict with others, having high rates of juvenile delinquency and a history of recurrent 'attempted suicide' (McCulloch, Philip, and Carstairs, 1967; Ovenstone and Kreitman, 1974). These individuals are in conflict with the community rather than isolated from it: they may be relevant to the gradual persistent increase in suicide rates in young adults which has occurred over the last fifteen years.

Wage earners in the United States (Dublin, 1963) have been less vulnerable to suicide than others over a period of fifty years and suicide rates have increased in severe economic crises both in the United States and in Great Britain during this century, affecting preferentially the upper and middle classes. Loss of status, prestige, and sense of purpose seem to be the important elements, because indigenous poverty does not seem in itself relevant (Sainsbury, 1955). Suicide falls dramatically during times of war when of course unemployment is minimal and the community has an increased aim and sense of purpose (Sainsbury, 1968). Suicide rates in immigrants are higher than those of their countries of origin, though some studies suggest that they still retain a high order of rank correlation with them (Sainsbury, 1968). Interpretation of suicides in immigrants is of course complicated by the possibility that vulnerable individuals preferentially choose to leave their country of origin. This may be an important factor even when emigration has occurred under strong political pressures (Mezey, 1960). The study of life events has been a particularly fruitful approach to our understanding of mental illness (Brown et al., 1973a, 1973b), and the findings that losses of various kinds are important in leading to depression, especially when they have a threatening significance, e.g. death, divorce, departures of family members, or events following interpersonal arguments (Jacobs, Prusoff, and Paykel, 1974), have implications for suicide in view of its close relationship with depressive illness. There is an increased risk of suicide in the four years after bereavement, more marked in men than in women (McMahon and Pugh, 1965). Suicides have also been found to have a significantly increased number of losses due to the death of a parent in the previous three years, especially loss of a mother (Bunch, et al., 1971b). In a series of seventy-five suicides, 24 per cent. were found to have experienced bereavement of a parent or spouse over the previous two years compared with 4.7 per cent. of controls (Bunch, 1972).

In confining our discussion to published data we have of course concentrated on social factors which can be most easily measured. There may well be many others which are of possible relevance to suicide but because of their abstract nature which makes them difficult to measure they have not been examined systematically. Such matters as attitudes of the community to death and suicide, and tolerance of others towards individuals with psychological difficulties or to those who find themselves in compromised situations over moral, sexual, financial, or other issues, may well be relevant because they govern the way in which society reaches out to the individual as opposed to excluding him when he gets into difficulties of various kinds.

Many of these issues are well illustrated by the circumstances which led to the suicide of Thomas Chatterton (1752–1770) whose literary genius revealed itself at an early age. Unfortunately he met little encouragement in Bristol, the city of his birth, and he became increasingly frustrated and angry at the limitations which the contemporary social situation imposed upon him. He received his keep but no salary, and was able to free himself from his apprenticeship only by writing a suicide note and his Will. These were penned three months before he eventually ended his life, and they are remarkable for the anger which they display. He referred to 'my pride, my damn'd native unconquerable pride, that plunges me into distraction'. In what must be one of the most remarkable of all suicide notes, Chatterton commented that 'the most perfect masters of human nature in Bristol distinguish me by the title of the Mad Genius', and he bequeathed to various people living there his vigour and fire of youth, his humility, prosody and grammar, his religion, power of utterance, and free thinking. To Bristol itself he left his spirit and disinterestedness as well as his debts. Chatterton committed suicide three months later at the age of 17 years, starving and penniless in London, still with a sense of outrage at a Bristol which was unable either to comprehend him or help him to break away from the working class social bonds in order to express his genius. Southey later attempted to soften the impact of Chatterton's death by noting that his sister had been confined for a time in an asylum for the insane, and so he inferred: 'His mighty mind brought with it into the world a taint of hereditary insanity, which explains the act of suicide, and divests it of its fearful guilt' (Wilson, 1869). Chatterton's suicide may more profitably be understood as a result of his progressive alienation from a society which could not understand him, leading eventually to a situation in which neither he nor others around him were able to compromise in thier basic assumptions and attitudes. His death illustrates important issues relevant to any serious study of suicide, and its impact has not lost its immediacy even though it occurred just over 200 years ago.

3.3 The Search for Causes

Individual and situational factors which we have discussed as concomitants of suicide cannot necessarily be assumed to have a causal significance, or if they do then at most this may be an indirect one. Most would agree than an individual's final decision to end his life is probably influenced by both his psychological state and the situation in which he finds himself, the one usually reinforcing the other regardless of which may have originated first. None of the concomitants which we have discussed is either necessary or sufficient as an explanation of suicide. To take depression as an example, not all suicides are depressed at the time they kill themselves and not all depressives end their lives. In fact all concomitants whether personal or situational have a very low level of predictive power, and the majority of individuals experiencing them do not commit suicide. We are forced to remind ourselves that each suicide is a highly personal and idiosyncratic act and we have to introduce the concept of predisposing psychological vulnerability which contributes to the way in which the individual reacts to a situation. This leads us to a further problem of assessing situational factors, namely the highly individual way in which we perceive stress. A life event may have catastrophic effects in one but another may escape from it unscathed, or paradoxically cope better than before.

Studies of social factors, especially when the ecological method is used (see Chapter 9 for a more detailed discussion of this technique), have been forced to concern themselves with relatively crude criteria because of limitations in available data; the resulting picture of the social situation is therefore restricted by the research method used. Thus Sainsbury's studies which stem from an ecological initiative have emphasized the stereotype of an older depressed isolate, whilst those from Edinburgh based on a Poisons Treatment Centre point to the increasing importance of chronic conflict with others and social chaos in younger persons who kill themselves. In each individual who commits suicide the causes are usually multiple and highly idiosyncratic. Nevertheless, it behoves us to make what we can of the known concomitants, whether we are therapists assessing individual risk or health planners deciding on the disposition and character of service resources.

3.4 Rational Suicide

Is self-destruction ever a justifiable decision, one taken by a normal individual who has carefully and rationally taken stock of his life? This is not just a philosophical question but one of immense importance to those who are faced with the problem of helping people in despair, for they need to decide whether to intervene or leave alone. If they do too little they miss a preventable suicide in someone who needs help, whereas if they are too vigorous in their intervention they may be guilty of unwarranted intrusion into someone else's personal and private affairs.

We can only discuss this problem in the context of present-day life because clearly at other times there have been marked variations in attitudes to suicide, particularly that which was altruistic and directed at the group as a whole. Our understanding is of course limited by the fact that available information about suicides is so often retrospective and deficient, even when they have been in contact with services shortly before their death. It does seem, however, that the more intensively we look, the greater amount of evidence we find for psychological disturbance, often of a depressive nature and probably present in more than 90 per cent. of cases during the weeks preceding the act. How many therefore should be regarded as being mentally ill? Frequently the disturbance is not recognized by those whom the suicide consults. This is of course a common situation in depressive illness when the patient may experience a very personal kind of suffering to be shared with none other. In certain individuals sudden severe changes of mood can occur form day to day, especially when alcohol acts as a precipitant, leading to suicidal impulses; there may then not have been evidence of psychological disturbance in the weeks before suicide occurred, though at the time of death their thought processes may have been as disturbed as in any depressive illness.

It is facts such as these that make it so difficult to comment upon the incidence of rational suicide. They also force the therapist to adopt a highly conservative approach in which it is assumed that whenever he has the opportunity he should try to prevent suicide, no matter how catastrophic the person's circumstances might appear. 'Balance sheet' suicide (*Bilanz-Selbstmord*) was a term coined by Hoche in 1919 (Choron, 1972) to describe a situation in which a person cooly and apparently rationally talks without obvious emotional distress of suicide in the face of severe life problems, e.g. intractible physical disease. Should we turn our heads and let things take their course on the assumption that we ourselves, in that situation, would feel the same way? Yet we know that our own intuitive judgements in such circumstances can be highly fallacious, and the individual may in reality be testing us out to determine whether we can offer hope; if we fail him in this respect his despair is likely to be confirmed and accentuated. The question whether suicide is ever rational forces us back onto our own individual assumptions about life—why we are here and why we want to go on with it—and there can be no definitive statement about this issue which would cover all possible views. It will be considered again later when we discuss suicide prevention.

4

TWELVE SUICIDES

Before proceeding to consider other aspects of suicide it is useful at this point to examine the problems which arose with regard to twelve persons who killed themselves whilst under the care of our clinical team. The difficulties which we experienced in our relationship with these patients will be seen to have relevance to suicide in general, and so they provide a useful way of setting the scene for our subsequent more detailed discussions.

The patients are all those who committed suicide during the period 1968–1978 and who did so either whilst currently under our care or within two months of clinical contact with us. Our findings are therefore based on a direct and immediate experience of the problems involved. Ten of them were regarded unequivocally as suicides by coroner inquest. Open verdicts were returned on the other two, but the clinical facts suggest that there is little doubt that death was by suicide: one had secretly left the ward and within a few hours was found drowned in a nearby river, whilst the other fell from a precipice at the point where she had been rescued some months before and from which she had repeatedly threatened to throw herself. Brief case histories will first be presented, followed by the problems which we experienced in their care. The patients are referred to by the letters A to M indicating their admission sequence. In the tables they are arranged in order of increasing age.

4.1 Case Histories

A. Female, 18 years old, single

After a stormy rebellious adolescence this young immature woman gave birth to a baby at the age of 17; a great deal of angry confrontation ensued with relatives, particularly her father, concerning its adoption. She became very upset when her cohabitee left her, and she then developed intense preoccupation with ideas of committing suicide by jumping off a local cliff. Four months before her death she had been admitted to a psychiatric ward following a dramatic rescue from the face of these same cliffs, an episode which made national news. Diagnosis: reactive depression, with adolescent behaviour disorder. She continued to talk openly, some felt in a boastful way, about her suicidal ideas and eventually she refused to stay in hospital. A few days later she was found dead at the foot of the cliffs about which she had talked so much, beneath the ledge from which she had previously been rescued.

B. Female, 35 years old, married

This woman developed a depressive illness six months after childbirth, some eighteen months previously. Treatment with antidepressant and tranquillizer drugs by her general practitioner did not resolve her problems; she was referred to us after having been ill for one year. She had always been a meticulous, obsessional woman, and her own mother had committed suicide. In her final illness she exhibited self-blame, and talked about ending her life and of putting her two children and her husband 'to sleep' as well. She had been episodically very tense, tending to scream in her distress and to be regarded as 'hysterical'. Although she improved considerably on the two occasions when she was admitted to hospital, on one occasion receiving a course of electroplexy, she relapsed on returning home. At times she expressed paranoid ideas of being experimented upon and put her hands to her ears as if she was hallucinated, though she denied this. Diagnosis: depressive illness and personality disorder. One weekend we were asked to see her in an Accident and Emergency Department where she had attended following self-inflicted full-thickness skin lacerations to both wrists. She and her husband resisted readmission to hospital and she gave reassurance about her suicidal intentions. A few days later she committed suicide by jumping off a suspension bridge.

C. Female, 50 years, married

This women had always been well until seven years previously, when she developed depressive ideas which persisted without significant remission until she killed herself. Her illness followed soon after several upsetting life events, which included the deaths of her father and close friend, and an extramarital affair which generated a considerable degree of guilt as well as fear of pregnancy and cancer. She also had an isolated major epileptic fit for which no organic cause was found. Subsequently she had been admitted to a psychiatric hospital on several occasions. Diagnosis: chronic depressive psychosis and hypochondriasis. Treatment which included electroplexy and antidepressant medication failed to cause any remission in her symptoms. She presented in an impassive, unemotional way, and held persistent ideas that she was dead, describing herself as 'a walking corpse with only the talking left'. Her ideas about the future were profoundly pessimistic and she talked openly about committing suicide by lying on a railway track. She killed herself in this way a short time after refusing readmission to hospital and having given us reassurance that she would come for help if matters deteriorated.

D. Female, 17 years, single

This Jamaican girl had grand mal epilepsy and was an unmarried mother who lived in difficult social conditions. There had been at least two years of angry, hostile, acting-out behaviour with episodes of depression and six deliberate overdosages of drugs. She gave birth to a second child but refused admission to a psychiatric ward and two months later committed suicide by drug overdosage.

E. Female, 66 years, single

This woman had shown evidence of depression with hypochondriacal fears since the age of 38 years. She was preoccupied with vague lower abdominal pains and talked of her fear of 'adhesions' after hemicol-ectomy many years before. She was an active member of her local church community, lived alone in a large house, her parents and only sister having died, and she had major financial worries. There had been three episodes of admission to our psychiatric ward. Diagnosis: chronic reactive depression and hypochondriasis. Drug treatment, and on one occasion electroplexy, had produced little change in her symptoms. She could not accept reassurance about her physical state and she became more upset when a close friend had to have an abdominal operation. A few months before her death she developed suicidal ideas which were alien to her because of her religious views, and she felt particularly guilty at having taken two previous overdoses, describing herself as 'an emptiness in the eyes of God'. She put considerable pressure on us to gain readmission as an inpatient, but it was considered important that she did not retreat into institutional hospital life. The day after an interview with us, when she appeared to accept a programme of day care, she killed herself by an overdosage of drugs.

F. Female, 60 years, married

This woman had been well until five years previously. She then developed temporal lobe epilepsy, the management of which was complicated by her episodes of bizarre behaviour, such as throwing herself downstairs or hanging upside down from the first floor bannisters in her home. Her general appearance declined: she no longer did the housework, her memory became poor, and she showed marked restlessness together with choreiform arm movements. The variability in her behaviour and its rather bizarre nature made her family and the hospital staff suspect that she was deliberately and consciously assuming her symptoms, though a progressive dementia was definitely present. She became increasingly dependent on the hospital ward and whilst she was a day patient she showed great reluctance to return home each evening. She appeared to be irritable rather than depressed, though she took two deliberate drug overdoses in the last three months of her life, finally dying from aspiration pneumonia complicating ingestion of a quantity of a patent domestic abrasive.

G. Female, 23 years, married

We were asked to see this 23 year old housewife whilst she was an inpatient in the general hospital. She had suffered grand mal epilepsy for some years together with chronic rheumatic carditis and was receiving long-term anticonvulsants as well as oral penicillin. She developed emotional outbursts and was suspicious as well as resentful towards those who were trying to help her. She talked of suicidal ideas, of voices telling her to end her life, and felt a burden and danger to others: she felt particularly guilty at her outbursts against her 3 year old son, saying that on one occasion she had almost strangled him in temper. There had also been a recent episode of amnesia lasting for several hours, apparently unrelated to any epileptic disturbance. Diagnosis: epilepsy, reactive depression, personality disorder, and hysterical reaction. She was transferred to our psychiatric ward where it remained impossible to establish a close trusting relationship with her. At no time was she prepared to discuss her marital difficulties or fears about life problems in general; her behaviour was regarded by the staff as childlike and sulking. At times she became very tense, screamed at the staff, and cut her wrists. Her blackouts were suspected as being non-organic in origin because true loss of consciousness was not observed. Her distress was extremely variable and she made alliances with patients who were similarly hostile to the staff. Little progress was made in hospital and eventually she reluctantly returned home to face the realities of her family difficulties. Subsequent conjoint sessions had been arranged with her husband, but within twenty-four hours of leaving hospital she took a fatal overdose of tablets.

H. Male, 20 years, single

He was first referred to our outpatient clinic two years previously because of his increasingly odd behaviour and his expressed idea that he might kill his stepmother. His father had remarried after his mother had left the family when the patient was aged 7. He obtained eight 'O' level grades at school but then showed a rapid deterioration in his academic performance, coincident with the development of auditory hallucinations, incongruous giggling, and episodes of vacant staring into space. Subsequently he was admitted to hospital on three occasions and his florid symptoms rapidly subsided on each occasion. He appeared to be suffering from a schizophrenic illness though his undoubted abuse of LSD and amphetamines raised the possibility of drug-induced psychosis. He later developed ideas of passivity whereby he felt controlled by other people and he believed that he could read their minds. Though his psychotic symptoms improved with hospitalization he remained highly provocative and his attitude to staff was uncooperative. He failed to conform to ward routine, e.g. by refusing to get up from bed, absenting himself without leave to return after drinking alcohol, distributing amphetamines to other patients, aggressive outbursts, and on one occasion an overt sexual assault towards a female nurse. In this way he alienated himself increasingly both from his family and hospital staff, who suspected that much of his behavioural disorder was under his voluntary control. He continued to play an excellent game of chess and he wrote poetry of quality and perception. During his illness he took four overdoses of drugs and on one occasion lacerated his chest with a knife. After being ill for two years he eventually improved dramatically following a course of electroplexy and intramuscular phenothiazines; at this time he even found himself a job. This did not last long because he soon defaulted appointments, discontinued intramuscular medication, and two months later died through an overdosage of drugs.

J. Female, 55 years, widowed

Admission was precipitated by a severe overdose of a sedative drug, causing her to be deeply unconscious and requiring intensive physical resuscitation in the general hospital. Following treatment of a complicating pneumonia she was transferred to the psychiatric ward because she was thought to be severely depressed and preoccupied with suicide. Diagnosis: depressive psychosis. Her relatives confirmed that she had been depressed for more than two years following the death of her husband; the drug overdosage occurred at a time when her only son was intending to move away and she had in fact left him a suicide note. In the psychiatric ward she denied depressive symptoms and she claimed that the overdosage was because she wished to draw attention to herself. She said testily during her admission interview 'you don't die from an overdose'. That night she awoke screaming and next day she disappeared from the ward to be found shortly afterwards drowned in a nearby river.

K. Female, 28 years, married

After an unsettled childhood when she was fostered in Scotland, this woman come to Bristol at the age of 18 years in order to seek out her real mother, but she felt rejected and then spent several years in a psychiatric hospital intensely dependent on the institution, lacking in confidence, and generally very immature in her behaviour, though not suffering from a major mental illness. Diagnosis: reactive depression and personality disorder. She eventually left hospital, made a very unhappy marriage, and had a baby. The relationship with her husband gradually deteriorated. She made increasing requests for recurrent readmission to hospital, though these were resisted in view of her previous intensive dependence and loss of confidence following a prolonged stay in a psychiatric ward. Her distress was variable; at times she was even happy and unconcerned when attending the ward as a day patient. There were episodes of screaming at night and dreams of having homicidal impulses towards her child. She took two overdoses of drugs, the second of which was fatal.

L. Male, 45 years, married

This man had experienced difficulties over many years, mainly related to his prolonged feelings of inadequacy in his marriage and at work. He had lost a leg after an accident six years before and subsequently his problems gradually gathered momentum. Severe left facial neuralgia followed an attack of herpes zoster, necessitating a trigeminal nerve root section, and he was prescribed powerful analgesics without much benefit. Diagnosis: reactive depression and personality disorder. He lost his job, his marital difficulties became increasingly severe, and he complained of impotence. Therapy was difficult because of his general feelings of anger and resentment about his life problems, together with his inability to compromise with regard to his marital situation. When his wife left him he became depressed and he neglected his personal care, taking three major overdoses of tablets, the third of which proved to be fatal.

M. Male, 58 years, divorced, living as single

This man had experienced recurrent psychiatric problems for some twenty-five years, usually in the form of depression with paranoid features. His wife had left him fifteen years previously and he had subsequently lived an isolated life working as a lift attendant. His illness had been complicated by a severe head injury leading to a mild visual agnosia: he had subsequently misidentified people during relapses in his illness. Several admissions to psychiatric hospitals had occurred. Diagnosis: schizoaffective psychosis. He was treated with phenothiazines. Final relapse appeared to date from discontinuation of intramuscular medication four months previously when he appeared to be fully well. He developed a depressive paranoid state once again and was admitted to hospital after having deliberately walked in front of a car, sustaining minor abrasions. He was agitated and restless, and he left the ward repeatedly, though on each occasion he returned spontaneously to reassure the staff that he had merely visited the shopping centre. Though he had been assessed by the ward doctor one hour previously, and at that time had denied suicidal ideas, he killed himself by jumping in front of a lorry outside the hospital gates.

4.2 General Characteristics (see Table 3)

The average age was 31.5 years (range 17–66). Nine patients were female and three male. Only three lived alone: two had done so for many years, but one had only recently been left by his family. Three had chronic epilepsy (in one associated with dementia and in another with chronic rheumatic carditis). One had post herpetic neuralgia and eye ulceration and had also lost a leg in an accident three years previously.

All had received psychiatric treatment from our team: two were currently inpatients and three were day patients; two others had been discharged from inpatient care a few days before they committed suicide; three had received inpatient treatment approximately one month before; and one, previously well known to us, had attended our outpatient clinic one week prior to committing suicide. One had not been under our care since twelve months previously, though she had been assessed on two occasions in that time, the last being two months before her death.

TABLE 3   Twelve suicides: general characteristics

Patient:	D	A	H	G	K	B	L	C	J	M	F	E
Age:	17	18	20	23	28	39	45	50	55	58	60	66
Sex:	Female	Female	Male	Female	Female	Female	Male	Female	Female	Male	Female	Female
Marital status:	Single	Single	Single	Mar.	Sep.	Mar.	Sep.	Mar.	Wid.	Div.	Mar.	Sep.
Significant physical disorder												
Epilepsy	*											
Other				*			*				*	
Psychosis												
Organic dementia											*	
Schizophrenic			*									
(? drug induced)												
Schizoaffective										*		
Depressive								*	*			
Significant depressive symptoms with self-blame	*	*		*	*	*	*			*		*
Major situational problems	*	*	*	*	*	*	*					*
Duration of psychiatric difficulties (years)	2+	2	2	2	1+	1+	6	7	2	25	5	30

Major psychiatric difficulties had been present for at least a year in all cases (range 1–5 years), often with a picture of progressive deterioration in the face of life difficulties. Psychotic illness other than depression occurred in only three: an 18 year old man whose schizophrenic symptoms may have been related to drug abuse; a 60 year old woman with organic dementia and temporal lobe epilepsy; and a 58 year old man who had a chronic schizoaffective psychosis following a head injury. Two showed evidence of severe psychotic depression in the absence of obvious situational difficulties. Seven had depressive symptoms and major life problems against which they were struggling with decreasing success.

Eleven had 'attempted suicide' previously. Patients D and H had taken overdoses repeatedly during the last two years, but in most patients these attempts were commonest during the last six months.

4.3 Problems of Management

Communication of suicidal ideas

All the patients had talked openly at some time during the last few weeks of their lives about feeling suicidal. Three accurately predicted the method which was eventually used in their self-destruction: A jumped from a very point on the cliff from where she had previously been rescued, M had jumped in front of a car a few days before he finally did so with fatal results, and C had talked openly about lying on a railway line before she killed herself in this way one week later.

Several factors appear to have complicated the assessment of suicide risk in these patients (Table 4). Eight of them stated quite explicitly when

TABLE 4 Twelve suicides: features influencing assessment of suicide risk

	D	A	H	G	K	B	L	C	J	M	F	E
Suicide intent												
Expressed openly	*	*	*	*	*	*	*	*	*	*	*	*
Reassurances given to staff	*		*			*		*	*	*	*	*
Marked variation in degree of distress	*	*	*	*	*	*						
Expressed anger towards others	*	*		*			*		*		*	
Regarded as being pro-vocative/unreasonable	*	*	*	*			*				*	

interviewed that they no longer felt suicidal and that they would come for help in a crisis. This seems to have occurred particularly in the older patients, and in all those over 50 years of age. In view of the fact that we knew most of these patients extremely well we felt that the contractual relationship would be effective and their reassurances could be accepted. This assumption may, however, have been rendered invalid by a situation of confrontation and conflict between patient and staff which developed in a considerable number of cases. Seven pressed for readmission and this was refused in an attempt to prevent a state of overdependence on the hospital. Their talk of suicide during these confrontations was seen as an angry threat which signified little or no risk. Reassurances in two (J and M) may have been an attempt to deceive the staff with regard to their real suicidal intentions, judging from their proximity to the suicide act, but in others they appeared to be due to a real ambivalence with regard to this issue.

Six showed marked variation in the degree of their distress and this led to a belief on the part of the staff that they were in fact sufficiently improved to be regarded as no longer at risk of suicide. Such marked variability was present in all patients under 40 years of age and in none of the six older than this. It was usually related to further exposure to the interactional difficulties which had been an integral part of their recent crisis: such patients were often relaxed and apparently well in the hospital ward. Perhaps the best example was K, who enjoyed a sponsored walk which she had organized around the hospital grounds one week before her suicide, which occurred after she had been discharged back to a marital situation which caused her great distress.

Six showed considerable anger directed towards others, a feature which appeared to be as marked as any depressive element. Perhaps because suicide is associated in out minds most commonly with inwardly directed aggression and self-blame, the irritable and difficult patient at real suicide risk seems less likely to be taken seriously.

Clinical features

Depressive symptoms were exhibited in ten patients with clear depression of mood and tearfulness as well as some degree of self-blame. In seven of these the picture was one of vulnerable individuals struggling with real life difficulties; only two (C and J) had severe psychotic depressive symptoms in the absence of any obvious situational difficulties. Patient M had a chronic relapsing schizoaffective illness. The diagnosis of schizophrenia was made in H, though his psychotic symptoms may have been due to hallucinogenic drug abuse. Patient F, a middle aged woman, showed evidence of early dementia together with epilepsy.

Marked physical restlessness and agitation was a striking feature in six patients. In L this occurred in the setting of his inability to accept compromise with regard to his marital difficulties, and he saw himself in an insoluble deteriorating social situation. During the two or three days before M committed suicide he disappeared from the ward on more than one occasion to return after an hour with reassurances about his intentions.

Five of these agitated patients also showed episodic screaming, in itself an unusual symptom: K would wake up screaming at night with recurrent dreams of killing her child, F used to scream inexplicably when with her husband, B would scream in the ward, on one occasion holding her hands over her ears as if aurally hallucinated, G rushed out of interviews screaming, shouting, and extremely tense, and J awoke screaming the night before she killed herself.

Relationship with others (see Table 5)

Six patients eventually found themselves in a situation whereby through their behaviour, which was regarded as provocative, difficult, and

TABLE 5 Twelve suicides: symptoms, behaviour, and relation to others

Patient	D	A	H	G	K	B	L	C	J	M	F	E
Depression with self-blame	*	*		*	*	*	*	*	*	*		*
Marked agitation				*	*	*	*			*	*	
Episodic screaming				*	*	*			*		*	
Loss of support from key others	*	*	*	*			*			*		
Staff critical	*	*	*	*	*		*				*	*
Confrontation with staff over dependency			*	*	*		*				*	*
Deliberate disability suspected by staff		*	*	*	*	*	*	*	*		*	*
Provocative and 'unreasonable'		*	*	*	*		*				*	

unreasonable, they had lost a great deal of sympathy and support from others. Patients D, A, G, and H were hostile and provocative at times when they did not appear to be depressed.

This impression that the patient was being unreasonable and perhaps deliberately uncooperative was particularly common in the younger patients, but in only one (F) over 45 years of age. Patient F earned this reputation through the bizarre nature of her symptoms, which included hanging by her feet upside down from the hall bannister at home, or at times running away screaming from her husband. In retrospect it seems likely that these were features of temporal lobe epilepsy and dementia, which if they had been fully recognized at the time might have produced a more sympathetic response from others.

Following major problems of management the staff eventually felt quite critical and indeed hostile towards eight patients. They found it difficult to accept that extreme variability in the degree of manifest distress, or hostile, angry, and acting-out behaviour was compatible with true suicidal intentions. Major confrontations over what was seen as unnecessary dependency on the hospital situation occurred in six cases.

In ten patients, the staff came to suspect that there may have been a degree of deliberate assimilation of symptoms merely to impress others. Bizarre symptoms or variability in distress appeared in particular to provoke this response to a patient with the result that suicide risk was taken less seriously. Patient A's open talk about suicide was seen as flamboyant and histrionic. Both F and G undoubtedly had epilepsy but it was difficult to distinguish acting out behaviour from it because no episodes of loss of consciousness occurred. It was difficult to assess L's facial pain when he was so upset about his marital problem. Patient H behaved quite outrageously at times, disobeying many of the ward rules and sexually assaulting a nurse, making it very difficult to assess his symptoms which at times were undoubtedly schizophrenic and bizarre. Patient C had talked for several years about being dead and she had not responded to intensive physical treatment, eventually being regarded as having a hysterical element in her illness. Episodes of screaming and agitation in B and angry outbursts in G raised suspicions that they were histrionic rather than suicidal.

4.4 Conclusions

What is the relevance of these findings to suicide in general? The series described in this chapter is small and in many ways different from the usual suicide stereotype. There is a preponderance of young women and no elderly males; the most common diagnosis was chronic depression in the face of major life difficulties and only two presented a typical picture of endogenous depression; none showed evidence of alcoholism. Serious chronic physical disease was uncommon, although three patients had chronic epilepsy. In spite of these considerations the findings from this series of suicides may well be more than idiosyncratic, and they have an immediacy which is heightened by the fact that they are derived from our direct experience in clinical care.

The progressive alienation of patient from effective help, as so often happened in this series, may well have a much wider significance. Indeed, the factor which contributed to a general feeling of therapeutic bankruptcy on the part of staff, and no doubt the patients as well, probably come into play in all problems involving behavioural difficulties which do not respond readily to repeated overtures of help. They may be relevant to a considerable proportion of all suicidal individuals both in the community, particularly in terms of family relationships, and in the hospital setting as described in this chapter.

Why was assessment so difficult?

Although traditionally the profound unremitting gloom of depressive psychosis has become the stereotype of high suicide risk the present series demonstrates that such a picture is not necessarily the most obvious one in persons who kill themselves. Whilst depressive symptoms were present in ten of the twelve patients, we were perhaps misled by other features which were present in addition. These included anger and resentment which seemed just as manifest as depression, as well as the problem of unusual, perhaps bizarre, symptoms which did not fit into any clear diagnostic category. Marked variability in the degree of distress, depending on the degree of contact with situational difficulties or from time to time in a ward situation, also proved to be a problem in assessment. This may go some way to explain the salutary fact that reassurances about suicidal intent were given to us so often, though we had known the patients extremely well over an extended period. At times these individuals presumably felt improved and were able to give positive assurances that they would not kill themselves, only to relapse very easily into despair, particularly when the precipitating situation recurred. In only two patients is it likely that reassurances were part of a deliberate deception, judging from the proximity between them and the act of suicide.

What were the management difficulties?

Quite clearly, most of the patients in this series progressively lost sympathy both from relatives and hospital staff alike through their inability to overcome their problems, and in some cases through their difficult behaviour. Attention was turned by staff increasingly from their unsatisfactory life situation onto the patients themselves and their responsibility for getting better: staff became critical and suspected the patients of deliberately assuming their symptoms. Eventually a confrontation arose over what was seen as unjustifiable dependency on the ward situation. Several patients killed themselves after being told that it was in their best interests to remain in the community. Was this policy correct?

This is probably one of the most important and difficult issues in the management of mental illness and behavioural problems. What criteria do we use in reaching a decision that an individual can and should cope without hospitalization? It is, of course, self evident that before making this judgement we should know our patient well and have full knowledge of the situational difficulties involved. We should also be sure that our attitude does not stem from angry rejection, and the patient should be assured of continued alternative kinds of support. Finally, we should ensure that our refusal to admit a patient is not based on administrative considerations. Factors such as shortage of beds should not be a basis for such a decision, and at a time when hospital facilities are being reduced in favour of those which are community based we must take care to be able to cater adequately for those who need a period of asylum from intolerable life difficulties.

The problems which may arise in the management of the suicidal have been emphasized by other studies (Farberow, Shneidman, and Neuringer, 1966; Flood and Seager, 1968), particularly the common occurrence of behaviour which is seen as hostile, manipulative, and demanding. In our own small series there was a striking relation between behaviour and age. Those patients over 45 years of age, though showing greater incidence of psychiatric symptoms, were more likely to cover up their suicidal behaviour. Younger patients tended more often to act out, to get into angry confrontations with others, and to be seen as provocative and unreasonable. This finding has a parallel with that from an Edinburgh study which has emphasized the way in which younger persons who eventually commit suicide commonly show a history of conflict with others and sociopathic behaviour leading to lives of increasing social chaos (Ovenstone and Kreitman, 1974). In our subsequent discussions on assessment and management of suicidal individuals we will need to keep in mind all such points illustrated by our series of twelve suicides.

5

ASSESSMENT OF THE SUICIDAL INDIVIDUAL

In this chapter we will consider the situation which arises when we find ourselves faced with an individual who may be in imminent danger of committing suicide. During the last month or so of their lives almost two-thirds of persons who proceed to kill themselves seek help from medical practitioners and other care agencies (Barraclough et al., 1974; Capstick, 1960; Robins et al., 1959; Seager and Flood, 1965). Our discussion will further show that a considerable proportion may talk quite clearly about their self-destruction intentions. It follows that we need to be skilled in recognizing those who are at serious risk of suicide and we must be able to relate to them in such a way that they receive every encouragement to accept help. The most effective evaluative technique is the direct face-to-face discussion with the person at risk, and it is to this we will now turn our attention.

5.1 The Interview Technique

Zeal in collecting facts should not detract from the need to encourage the patient to feel at ease: if the interview takes the form of an interrogation, much of what is important will be missed. On the other hand, a systematic approach helps. The best compromise is to have in one's mind a checklist of important areas which need to be covered, though the exact sequence in which this is done will vary depending on the way the patient wishes to participate in the discussion. The patient may be guarded and in some degree unwilling to communicate his feelings fully, especially at the first meeting. Our task is to create a situation whereby the suicidal individual can declare the full degree of his despair, whether this be unremitting or episodic, and in spite of his doubts about whether it is useful to do so.

The current situation

It is best to begin by discussing the immediate crisis. In a relaxed yet interested and sympathetic way we ask the patient simply to tell us of his recent difficulties and his feelings about them. It may be useful from the start to say that we recognize his distress and that we are concerned to accept, understand, and help rather than judge and pronounce. Certain interpersonal or social stresses are particularly common in the suicidal; they include social isolation, estrangement from others, all kinds of loss, whether in the form of bereavement, or concerning finance, status, esteem, separation, divorce, or religious belief. Also closely related are psychological conflicts and intolerance on the part of others with regard to personal problems.

In an emergency situation it may be sufficient to be guided by the patient's evaluation of these factors, though this may be far from a more objective assessment which may be obtained by interviewing 'key others' or a home visit.

Background history

It can be very difficult in the crisis situation to gain a picture of an individual's early years of childhood, and indeed it is best initially to confine enquiry to those areas which can be seen by him as having immediate relevance to his present problems. Someone who is suicidal is only too ready to dismiss the helper as being unable to remedy a hopeless situation, and avoidance of irrelevant issues is essential.

Chronic painful illness, especially when it is a source of anxiety and depression, can be a central issue. The emotional upset of hypochondriasis when there may be little evidence of organic disease may of course be just as significant in the crisis situation.

The problems inherent in the assessment of previous personality are enormous in someone who is contemplating suicide because the view of the self is often grossly distorted by the emotional disturbance. The useful form of questioning such as 'how would you describe yourself as a person before your difficulties began?' may evince morbid comments such as 'I've always been hopeless, a sham and a fraud', though in themselves these are important as a measure of the degree of present disturbance. The personality attributes which may be relevant to our assessment include impulsivity, spontaneous depressive swings of mood, use of alcohol or other agents which may affect impulsivity and mood, aggressive tendencies, rigidity and inability to adjust to new situations, attitudes to death, and religious conviction. Whilst a strong faith can be a protection against suicide, its loss, together with the development of suicidal ideas, can also be a source of great guilt. One of our suicides, following previous overdoses of tablets, described her loss of religious faith and her belief that she had now become a 'gap in the eyes of God'. Assessment of personality is important because it provides the baseline of psychological norm for the particular individual, thereby permitting assessment of the degree of change which has occurred, its rate of development and possible idiosyncratic impact of life events depending upon his individual strengths and vulnerabilities. Discussion of these issues with a key 'other person' is well worthwhile, taking care of course to obtain the patient's prior permission.

Enquiry about previous psychiatric illness may produce information of direct relevance to the present crisis. When a series of major breakdowns have occurred they may in any individual be remarkably stereotyped with regard to their nature, causation, and outcome, and hence of predictive value regarding the precise significance of any current disturbance.

Assessment of mental state

Following discussion of the patient's history it is conventional to attempt some systematic evaluation of his current psychological function. This of course is merely an extension of the same interview, though it is wise to make the purpose of any simple tests of psychological function which may be used fully explicit to the patient.

Whatever the diagnostic category of the underlying disturbance, it seems clear that a disorder of mood is the most common finding in persons who are about to commit suicide. The symptoms recorded as observed in more than 20 per cent. of the hundred unselected suicides studied by Barraclough *et al.* (1974) are listed in Table 6. Virtually all these patients were judged to have been mentally ill, confirming the previous studies from St. Louis (Robins *et al.*, 1959) and Seattle (Dorpat and Ripley, 1960). It follows that it must be rare for the suicidal individual to be completely asymptomatic, and a skilled evaluation of the mental state is essential. Our own series of suicides emphasizes the day-to-day variability in degree of distress which may be observed in those who commit suicide, particularly when they ate temporarily removed from the major stress in their lives. Apparent improvement following self-harm or during the early stages of treatment such as ECT can also be fragile and deceptive. We must be careful not to accept reassurances concerning suicidal intent too readily merely because of what may be a temporary break in the clouds of despair.

TABLE 6 Symptoms of 100 suicides recorded during four weeks prior to death in 20 per cent. or more of patients

	Depression $N=64$ %	Alcoholism $N=15$ %	Miscellaneous $N=14$ %	Not mentally ill $N=7$ %	All $N=100$ %
Looked miserable	89	40	43	0	69
Insomnia	86	80	50	29	76
Taking hypnotics	70	73	43	29	64
Weight change	69	67	57	57	66
Looked anxious	67	53	43	29	60
Complained of sadness	64	60	14	14	53
Weight loss	61	47	43	43	53
Difficulty in working	61	33	21	0	47
Reduction in work	53	53	43	0	48
Less interest	53	40	29	14	45
Pessimistic or hopeless about future	52	47	21	0	43
Anorexia	50	60	21	0	44
Less social activity	47	27	43	0	40
Less energy	47	33	29	0	39
Slower movements	45	40	43	14	42
Reproached self	44	40	7	14	36
Difficulty in concentrating	42	33	21	0	35
Weeping	42	60	14	14	39
Restless	41	40	14	0	34
Diurnal mood variation	38	20	43	0	30
Hypochondriacal	36	53	7	14	35
Indecisive	33	20	7	0	25
Thought self a burden	33	20	29	14	29
Slower speech	31	40	57	0	34
Useless or worthless	31	33	14	0	27
Thought let people down	28	27	7	0	23
Complained of anxiety	28	40	43	14	31
Trembling/shaking	22	53	14	0	24

Source: Barraclough et al., 1974.

All studies have emphasized the importance of certain high-risk psychiatric syndromes, and the problems encountered in the evaluation of these will now receive particular attention.

Affective illness. Almost two-thirds of any unselected sample of suicides will have shown evidence of depressive illness in the weeks prior to their death. The incidence of depression increases with age. The recent study of Barraclough *et al.* (1974) showed that 75 per cent. of depressive suicides are over 45 years of age. Depressives who kill themselves were also found to have attempted suicide far more often than a control series of living depressed patients (46 compared with 6 per cent.). The frequency of symptoms which were found in this diagnostic group are found in Table 6. An earlier study in St. Louis (Robins *et al.*, 1959) described a similar clinical picture, emphasizing insomnia, weight loss, anorexia, and depression of mood. In both studies pessimism regarding the future (in less than 53 per cent.) and various forms of self-blame or guilt (in less than 44 per cent.) were not by any means the most frequent symptoms, indicating that these are not necessarily features of depression which lead to suicide, at least not those which are easily observed by relatives and friends.

The interview with a severely depressed individual may present several practical problems, mainly due to the distortion of reality testing. If all hope has been lost then there may be deliberate evasion and denial of suicidal intent; the interview will be seen as a waste of time and the interviewer regarded as misguided or lacking in understanding. It is crucial therefore that we should adopt an appropriate attitude to this situation. We need to recognize despair, and as soon as possible to indicate that we have done so. This may in itself be of enormous benefit in giving the patient confidence and trust in someone who might be able to understand. It is essential to avoid trivial reassurances, no matter how tempting it is to do so, because these only confirm fears of not being taken seriously or that nobody can appreciate the true degree of distress: in fact, we need only to confirm and emphasize our determination to help and understand. If we remember that the patient may be preoccupied with self-blame, then we will avoid casual comments and generalizations which are liable to be misinterpreted in a way which reinforces morbid guilt and feelings of being a burden. Litman and Farberow (1961) have emphasized the serious picture of feeling helpless, hopeless, and of exhaustion and failure. Sometimes the patient attempts to get us to join in his despair, e.g. by suggesting that no further appointments are necessary because things will always be the same. As we know that depression usually has a finite duration it is important to refuse to go along with this kind of thinking, and to explain why.

Chronic alcoholism and drug addiction. This is second in importance only to depressive illness as a causative factor in suicide, being the principal diagnosis in 15 to 23 per cent. of suicides. The incidence of various symptoms in this diagnostic group as found by Barraclough *et al.* (1974) are listed in Table 6. Heavy drinking had occurred in all cases in this group and it is striking that depressive symptoms were also very common, though at a lower frequency than in patients judged to have depressive illness as the principal diagnosis. Only a very small number were confused (13 per cent.) or deluded (13 per cent.), and none were hallucinated, so it appears that organic withdrawal states were not prominent. Depression may of course ensue when an addicted individual attempts to withdraw from alcohol and especially when his drinking has led to major difficulties in his social and personal life. A previous history of attempted suicide was far more common in alcoholics who committed suicide (66 per cent.) than in others (10 per cent.).

The mistrust which addiction produces, both on the part of the patient and in those who try to help, accentuates the problems of assessment when an individual with alcohol or drug dependence becomes seriously depressed and suicidal. Gross disregard for personal welfare, especially concerning drug dosage or observance of sterile techniques when injection is used, may be important indicators of depression, especially if these are new developments. The risk of severe depression in suicide is high when amphetamines are stopped suddenly, and as a result it is usual to offer hospital admission routinely in these circumstances.

Schizophrenia can be very difficult to assess from the point of view of suicide risk: it is likely that a high proportion of unexpected suicides are due to it. In its early stages, presumably when insight is retained into bizarre and frightening symptoms such as auditory hallucinations or delusional ideas, it is particularly likely that depression and despair will follow. During interview, therefore, it is essential to explore whether psychotic symptoms of this kind have been present and sometimes there are clues to be found in the patient's behaviour: he may have been unexpectedly suspicious, hostile, or even aggressive to others, or there may be indirect evidence of auditory hallucinations, when he might have been observed tense and distressed, perhaps holding his hands over his ears. Such indirect clues are important when psychotic symptoms make it unlikely that the patient will talk openly about his innermost fears, not the least his suicidal ideas. When hallucinations and delusional ideas are clearly related in their content to suicide then they must be taken particularly seriously.

Organic brain syndromes may also mean a high suicide risk, especially in the early stages of the illness, again presumably before insight is lost and when the patient still has the ability to evaluate the true significance of progressive intellectual deficit, mainly in the form of recent memory deterioration. When this is found together with severe depressive symptoms it is necessary to give serious consideration to suicide risk.

Epilepsy carries an increased risk of suicide when it is complicated by mood disorder such as depression and anger, especially in the setting of interpersonal and social difficulties which cannot be resolved easily. The risk is increased further if in the face of these problems the patient is reacting in an impulsive and emotionally labile way. The ready access which an epileptic has to potentially lethal drugs adds to the risk of deliberate overdose when a crisis occurs.

Personality disorder may mean that an individual has been in conflict with those around him for some time, and the presenting symptoms may be those of anger and resentment as much as depressive. Gross lability of mood, impulsiveness, and testing-out behaviour, so common in adolescence, should be seen objectively and not made the excuse for our angry rejection. Bagley (1975) has emphasized the importance of eliciting suicidal ideation which is significantly correlated with poor self-esteem, depression, and social withdrawal in both boys and girls. Our own series demonstrates how individuals who are in conflict with others may eventually find themselves deeply alienated from any means of help before they commit suicide.

Non-fatal deliberate self-harm. Those individuals who have taken overdoses or injured themselves in some other way non-fatally also constitute an important and common high-risk group. Their assessment will not be considered further at this point but will be deferred until later when it will be dealt with in the context of non-fatal deliberate self-harm.

5.2 The Communication of Suicidal Intent

In the St. Louis study of Robins *et al.* (1959) relatives and friends of 134 consecutive cases of suicide were interviewed in order to determine the way in which suicidal intentions had been communicated to others. The striking findings that over two-thirds (69 per cent.) had communicated suicidal ideas (41 per cent. of the entire group making their intentions clear) dispels the myth that those who kill themselves do not warn others before doing so. Such communications are repeatedly verbalized, diverse in content, and may be expressed to many different persons in the week preceding the suicide. Remarks of this kind are particularly ominous when they are atypical for the person concerned, especially when his general manner and behaviour are also unusual. A clear threat does not appear to be necessarily a more serious predictor of suicide than is an oblique hint; in fact the reverse may be so. Such messages may reflect a true mental conflict between the wish to die and the wish to live: they may be primarily coercive or a real 'cry for help' (Barraclough *et al.*, 1974).

The content of suicide notes can have relevance to the assessment of suicide risk, for example when found before suicide has occurred or when a 'suicide attempt' is survived. At the Los Angeles Suicide Prevention Center (Shneidman, 1976; Shneidman and Farberow, 1957) a detailed analysis of suicide notes has been carried out involving blind comparison with simulated ones. The genuine ones were significantly more verbose and contained a greater number of 'neutral statements' by which orders, admonitions, and lists of things to do are given as if the writer is thinking illogically about being absent yet giving instructions as though he were going to be around to enforce them. The larger number of neutral statements in the genuine notes—wherein reputation, or the self as experienced by others, is the primary characteristic—would seem to imply this paradox. The 'discomfort statements' which were found more often in genuine notes showed deeper feelings of hatred, vengeance, and self-blame. It seems that those notes which show the greatest concern for subsequent events with evidence of angry resentment may indicate the highest risk.

In view of these findings it may well be that during direct interview it should be possible to get a very high proportion of suicidal individuals to discuss their ideas concerning self-destruction. There is no evidence at all to suggest that open discussion will in any way increase the risk of suicide, though this erroneous idea is probably still widely held. We do of course need skills in learning how to lead into the topic of suicide ideation. Perhaps the best way is first to register that one recognizes the patient's distress and to ask in general terms whether he has felt despairing; if so, we then enquire whether he has reached the stage of not wanting to go on with life and whether actual suicide has been contemplated. Not infrequently, sympathetic enquiry helps the patient to cathartic relief of emotion at being able to share these appalling ideas with someone who may be able to understand and perhaps help.

As a general rule it is unwise to ignore talk about suicide. When the underlying reason is clearly related to psychotic thinking, such as depressive morbid self-blame and hopelessness, or schizophrenic or delusional ideas, then the risk of suicide is immediate and severe. Scrupulous care is demanded when such a patient expresses homicidal ideas, especially when the content is congruent with other psychotic beliefs. Sometimes talk of suicide is used recurrently in a superficial and manipulative way in the absence of any evidence of mental illness. Before we can dismiss it as having no life-threatening implications, however, we need to know the patient extremely well over an extended period of time: even then it may be wrong to dismiss it as unimportant, especially when significant depressive symptoms are present or alcohol abuse has been a cause of impulsive behaviour.

5.3 Some Special Assessment Difficulties

Concealment of suicidal ideas

Although a great many clearly do so, not all suicidal individuals will reveal their true intentions. Presumably those who conceal their feelings in this way are determined to kill themselves, come what may. We should be suspicious that such may be the case if the patient is evasive when questioned directly about suicidal intent, dodging the question and giving ambiguous replies. In these circumstances it is necessary to insist on a direct answer to such questions as 'do you think there is any danger that you might end your life?' or 'have you recently had ideas of committing suicide?'. An individual at risk will usually also show other symptoms which might suggest that psychological disturbance such as depression or alcoholism continues unabated. If it is thought that the patient can go home to re-attend for an early appointment, a useful strategy is to ask whether he is prepared to promise to seek help urgently in the interim period if things get worse. Failure to make this undertaking should be taken seriously, especially when one knows the patient well and a good relationship has previously been established with him.

When an individual who denies suicidal ideas shows behaviour which is inconsistent with this, such as having left a suicide note which suggested sustained intent and preparation for death, or having engaged in serious life-endangering behaviour, then we should be particularly careful not to accept reassurance easily.

The symptom-free

A proportion of those who are at serious risk of suicide may appear at interview to be symptom-free, relaxed, and optimistic. It is important not to take this at face value. Sometimes there is marked variability in the degree of distress, particularly when depression is closely related to situational factors and when alcohol abuse causes recurrent crises. Assessment must therefore be based not only on the symptoms elicited at interview but also those experienced in crises in recent weeks. The suicidal person very commonly feels markedly ambivalent about ending his life, and when he finally reaches the interview he may find a new confidence and be tempted to play down the seriousness of his intent. Alternatively, we may be faced with a 'smiling depression' where the individual can for short periods dissociate conscious feelings from those of inner despair, and so present a superficial air of normality. In this case sympathetic but careful and relevant questioning often punctures the veneer of unconcern, with the result that desperate feelings are then discussed openly with a sense of relief. Finally, it is important not to be reassured too easily by the symptomatic improvement that may occur following self-overdosage of drugs or self-laceration. Caution is indicated, particularly when severe depressive symptoms such as morbid self-blame and marked insomnia have been present in the recent past.

The hostile, difficult, and demanding

Our own series of hospitalized suicides demonstrate how a state of conflict and alienation may develop between a suicidal patient and staff, especially when difficulties have been intractible and causative factors could not be resolved easily. Judging from the findings of other investigators (Farberow, Shneidman, and Neuringer, 1966; Flood and Seager, 1968) such a development is not unusual in suicidal individuals, at least in those who receive treatment in hospital. It is therefore necessary to remember that some patients whom we see as complaining, demanding, controlling, troublesome, or whom we suspect may 'put on' symptoms, will kill themselves. It is important that we should be aware of our own reactions which may cloud our judgements in such situations.

Attitudes towards those at risk of suicide

Not infrequently when an individual is difficult or unresponsive to help we begin to feel that he 'threatens' suicide and we think we are being manipulated or controlled by his talk of self-destruction. Arising out of this interpretation we may lose sympathy and feel angry with him, believing that adequate self-control is well within the individual's reach if only he so chooses: in fact, we often underestimate the true strength of suicidal motivation. The more sure we are of ourselves and our judgement the less likely we are to react in this way. We may be tempted to resort to

62

reasoning such as 'do you realize what you are doing to your family by causing them all this worry?' or 'you've got a good home, why behave in this way?'. Such an approach merely confirms the fears of a suicidal individual that nobody really understands the true depth of his despair. When difficulties are prolonged and crises are recurrent we may incline to the view that the individual has a right to commit suicide and we begin to withdraw our efforts to help. In fact, no matter how chronic or severe the problem, we have no alternative but to continue helping to our utmost ability because we know that even the most severe depression has an end and that apparently insuperable life difficulties can change with time. Any loss of interest on our part may be the last straw and could tip the balance in favour of suicide. We will return to this later when treatment and prevention are discussed.

6

MANAGEMENT OF SUICIDE RISK

If the initial evaluation technique has been correct then it will have paved the way for appropriate management of an individual at risk of suicide. The task now is to get him to agree to accept help. To do this we have to formulate a plan in which goals seem practical, feasible, and relevant to the individual's particular problems.

6.1   Agreeing a Contract

If suicide risk is judged to be severe and help is refused then it may be necessary to insist on compulsory admission to a psychiatric unit. This may arise, for example, when depressive symptoms have reached psychotic severity, the individual expresses continuing suicidal ideas, and he cannot give any guarantee about whether he will act on them, particularly when he is not well known to us. The problems which may ensue in the supervision of such severe suicidal risk are dealt with later in this chapter. We will first concern ourselves with the management of those who agree to accept help and can therefore enter into a contractual relationship with a helper. What conditions should be fulfilled on both sides in such a helping relationship?

From the outset it is important that the patient should understand fully the nature, extent, and limits of the help being offered. Many will hesitate to commit themselves to a programme which is ill explained, but most will accept eagerly one which emphasizes the 'listening to' and 'being with' role of the therapist. Interviews which last longer than an hour are generally inadvisable: whilst it is important to let the patient ventilate his problem freely it is nonetheless crucial to discourage too much irrelevant discussion which not only clouds the main problems but confuses and fatigues both the therapist and patient. The duration of therapy cannot of

63

course be defined at its outset: it must proceed through a series of stages, the first of which is to remove the patient's despair and to restore his hope. Subsequent goals are successively set by mutual agreement in the light of what has already been achieved.

How readily available should the therapist be in this early crucial stage of the helping process? If suicide risk is present and it has been agreed that the patient need not be admitted to hospital then help should be readily available at any time, as a crisis may well occur before the next appointment. The use of lifeline strategies is of great value in this situation and they should be discussed before the end of the first interview. An invitation to make telephone contact with the therapist, one of his therapeutic team, or a hospital ward, if he himself is not available, can itself be a considerable source of support. Rarely is this offer abused. Such lifelines are likely to be more effective if they facilitate contact with persons known to the suicidal individual: in general he will be reluctant to contact strangers when he is in crisis.

6.2 Basic Elements of Psychotherapy

Whatever may be the underlying cause of the suicidal state the therapist should always follow certain basic principles in his approach to the patient and these must be observed even when special therapeutic techniques such as physical treatments are required in addition. We often forget the utmost importance of the basic ingredients of the helping process. They depend to a great extent on our own expressed concern, our ability to empathize, and our non-judgemental acceptance of the patient and his problems. Without doubt we differ greatly one from the other in our ability to achieve this approach, and many find it difficult to accept that constructive listening, a willingness to share problems in a structured, well-defined relationship, a determination to see the difficulties through, and a refusal to despair, are in their own right the most powerful of all therapeutic tools. The therapist who has a degree of native wit in this direction is probably far more effective than one who though he may bristle with theoretical knowledge has not learnt to relate in this way. Suicidal individuals often feel that they cannot share their painful feelings and distress with their family, and it can be a source of relief to find that someone else is prepared to listen without necessarily professing to do anything active in return. One patient in a quite unsolicited way expressed regular relief from such interviews saying 'I find it helpful because I come here, warts and all, yet still feel that I can unburden myself without being rejected'.

Such an approach can often be sufficient to produce symptomatic improvement and so may help to initiate an ongoing series of meetings in order to look more systematically at the problems involved. When this is achieved, it is sensible to spend time initially in a more detailed discussion of various aspects of the patient's symptoms and the way he sees his situation. The very clarification of what is happening may reduce the problem down to size and make it appear less enormous from the patient's viewpoint. During this process it is made clear that the therapist is a listener and he will not eventually produce oracular pronouncements: at all points it is assumed that the solution will eventually be found by the patient himself. Endless ongoing circuitous discussions must be avoided because not only do they tend to lead to disillusion on the part of both the therapist and patient but they carry the danger of producing a state of dependence on the part of the patient with resulting loss of confidence, which could in itself prove to be disastrous in the long run.

Following the initial stage of elaboration and definition of the problem it may be possible, particularly when symptomatic improvement has occurred, to proceed to a more radical attempt to resolve the situation which may be causing the disturbance. It is of course very difficult to distinguish between problems which are secondary to the patient's disturbed mental state and those which may have anteceded it and hence could be causal. Thus an irritable, depressed individual may eventually be in conflict with close relatives, when previously his family relationships had not presented problems. The significant other persons can profitably be asked to come along to be seen with the patient, or separately in order to define the situation further and perhaps pave the way for further ongoing discussions which attempt to resolve interpersonal problems. It may be appropriate to evaluate other issues in more detail, such as physical symptoms to exclude physical disease which the patient fears, but here again it is necessary to remember that a depressed individual may be secondarily hypochondriacal. Such investigations should be taken only as far as the usual medical criteria dictate and they should not be carried out merely to reassure the patient; if done for this reason alone they rarely reassure and can even accentuate anxieties.

The initial stages of such intervention often produce gratifying symptomatic improvement. Hope is regenerated and problems are reduced to realistic proportions through their systematic and objective review. It may be possible to avert a major crisis altogether, whether by a change in outlook on the part of the patient or by a reorganization of his relationships with key others in his life. Not infrequently, however, the initial therapeutic momentum slows down: problems remain in spite of thorough scrutiny, and perhaps as a result they appear to be more insuperable than before. What strategies are open to us in this situation?

If goals have been set in a realistic way and the therapist has avoided the pitfalls of being too directive, e.g. by promising recovery in an authoritative way during the initial interviews, then such a situation of therapeutic frustration is less likely to occur. The emphasis should be at all times on the value of relating and sharing the problem and the therapist should have the view that a solution will eventually be found: support must continue until this happens. At this stage a patient might suggest termination of therapy, and such a request must be scrutinized carefully. It may be that recovery has occurred and the reasons given are consistent with this. On the other hand, the patient may still be depressed, wishing to discontinue because of morbid ideas of futility, and so he tests out the therapist to ascertain whether this is his view too. In such circumstances we should respond with a firm affirmation of the value of continuing, with an expressed conviction that there will eventually be an end to his despair. The enormous psychological and recuperative powers which may come into play over the course of time, even in spite of continuing life difficulties, allow us this optimism.

Nevertheless, it is very important not to indulge in glib and facile reassurance in such a way that the patient feels that the true depth of his despair is not understood. The very depressed may find it impossible to believe in any reassurance, but still can be comforted by another's confidence and support. The temptation to try and change a depressed person's gloom and pessimism by reasoned argument clearly has a long history. Henri de Mondeville (1270–1325) advised: 'Keep up your patient's spirits by music of viols and ten stringed psaltery, or by forged letters describing the death of his enemies, or by telling him that he has been elected to a Bishopric, if a churchman.' Such a strategy is as unlikely to succeed now as it was when first advised seven hundred years ago.

Another important reason for failure to initiate treatment or to make any headway with it may lie in the attitudes and mental state of the patient himself. Anger and resentments which impair his ability to look at the situation objectively are common obstacles. The result is an extremely rigid and possibly prejudiced view of his problems. One of our suicides (L) presented this attitude when conjoint therapy was attempted with his wife: though a great deal of symptomatic improvement had occurred as a result of the initial stages of our intervention he remained unable to compromise or to identify with his wife's attitude, and this seemed to stem from a personality trait which had long been present irrespective of depressive crises. Anger is of course itself an important motive force in suicide. In his study of black suicide in the United States, Hendin (1969) has highlighted the importance of such chronic anger in a wider sense, reflecting the difficulties which face a minority group in a multiracial society.

Occasionally the hindrance to effective treatment is psychotic mental illness, in which the patient's view of his situation and those around him is grossly disturbed by delusional ideas and other psychotic symptoms into which he has no insight. It is very important indeed to detect this in the first evaluative interview because it often indicates a high suicide risk. Early recognition of psychosis also allows the necessary physical treatments to be initiated quickly. Detailed and prolonged discussion aimed at producing insight is highly inappropriate during the acute stages of psychotic illness and indeed could be dangerous if it delays the use of physical treatments. The most common psychotic disturbance in suicidal individuals is of course that related to severe depression with self-blame, nihilism, and despair. This may be difficult to detect because it does not lead to florid behavioural disorders and indeed may not be volunteered by the patient. On the other hand, the paranoid psychotic is usually suspicious and perhaps angry, and careful questioning may reveal his bizarre ideas of persecution, though he too is often very reluctant to talk about them. Organic psychoses, characterized by episodes of confusion and delirium, cause difficulties because of subsequent annesia for the event. Thus an alcoholic may not remember the fears of delirium tremens and so he is inclined subsequently to dismiss its significance although acutely disturbed and at great risk during each episode. As a general rule psychotic symptoms mean that an individual who is suspected as being at risk of suicide should be assessed by a psychiatrist without delay.

6.3 Physical Treatments

Drug therapy

The recent British study of Barraclough *et al.* (1974) examined the prescribed medical treatments of suicides at the time of their deaths (see Table 7).

It appears that a high proportion of suicides have currently been prescribed a wide range of psychotropic drugs. The authors comment on certain irregularities: only half of the depressives received antidepressants, the average dose of which was well below the recommended, or the drug had been continued for many months without clear effect;

TABLE 7 Prescribed medical treatment for 100 suicides at time of death

	Depression N = 64 %	Alcoholism N = 15 %	Miscellaneous N = 14 %	Not mentally ill N = 7 %	All N = 100 %
Prescribed psychotropic drugs	81	87	100	43	82
Barbiturates	53	53	57	43	53
Antidepressants	30	7	7	—	21
Phenothiazines	20	20	36	—	21
Calcium carbimide (Abstem)	—	7	—	—	1
Minor tranquillizers	23	20	21	—	21
ECT	5	—	7	—	3
Haloperidol	2	—	—	—	1
Hypnotics	70	73	43	29	64

Source: Barraclough *et al.*, 1974.

barbiturates, phenothiazines, and minor tranquillizers appeared to be overprescribed; phenothiazines, especially depot preparations in patients other than those with schizophrenia, may have had an overall harmful effect by contributing to the depressed mood state.

In a more detailed analysis of drug use in their series of suicides (Barraclough *et al.*, 1971) these authors also emphasized the fact that some patients with depressive illness were not treated by antidepressants and they conclude that a proportion would still be living had these drugs been used. They suggest that general practitioners have difficulty in recognizing depressive illness and in treating it effectively. They emphasized the danger of prescribed barbiturates, overdose of which in 1968 accounted for 30 per cent. of suicide verdicts and 65 per cent. of all suicide deaths due to drugs in England and Wales.

This particular study has been described in detail because it raises several important issues concerning the use of prescribed psychotropic drugs. It is clear that barbiturates are the most dangerous and their use in the treatment of insomnia should be severely restricted; the use of phenothiazines in patients other than schizophrenics also seems to be unsatisfactory. But can we accept the author's view that wider recognition of depressive illness, leading to a greater use of antidepressant drugs, would constitute a major advance in suicide prevention? There is good reason why we should only give qualified support to this approach.

Control trials certainly provide evidence that these drugs are effective in depression and all are agreed that if they are to be used they should be given as a planned course of treatment in adequate doses. In the great majority of depressive states, however, some situational causative factor is also relevant; simply ringing the changes or increasing the doses of antidepressant drugs may be of no effect and paradoxically may facilitate suicide by making the patient feel that yet another treatment approach has failed. The efficacy of antidepressants may be related to whether the patient is isolated or is receiving adequate social support, or to the degree of interpersonal conflict. We need to know much more about these issues before the true value of antidepressants in the suicidal person can be assessed. Poor response to such drug therapy is just as much an indication to review the kind of psychotherapy and social situation as it may be to readjust levels of antidepressive medication. It should also be pointed out that these drugs are not without their own serious side effects and can themselves be used as the means of suicide.

Electroconvulsive therapy

Though empirical in nature there is substantial evidence that electroconvulsive therapy (ECT) is an effective treatment in severe depression. It is at least as effective as antidepressant medication and it exerts its effects more rapidly (Royal College of Psychiatrists, 1977).

Most clinicians turn to ECT at an early stage of management when there is a severe suicide risk in depression. In such circumstances it is generally regarded as unsafe to await the results of antidepressant drug therapy which may in any case not lead to improvement before a delay of a week or more. It must be recognized that there is a strong and widespread reaction in the community at large against the use of ECT which has, for example, been dubbed a 'suspect' treatment by the National Association for Mental Health (MIND, 1975). Undoubtedly if it is abused through indiscriminate and excessive use then ECT is harmful, but it remains a valuable source of relief for several depressed, suicidal individuals and its administration is not in general accompanied by any significant degree of discomfort.

6.4   Some Particular Problems of Management

Managing the severe suicide risk

When assessment suggests that an individual is in imminent danger of committing suicide and suicidal motivation overrides any wish to accept help, then the usual policy is to arrange admission to a psychiatric unit immediately, if necessary by the use of compulsory procedures. What are the problems which may ensue in management and, in particular, what precautions can be taken to minimize the chance that suicide will occur?

Although some authors have emphasized the importance of intensive surveillance and security in a closed psychiatric ward as a major factor in suicide prevention (Robins *et al.*, 1959) others emphasize different strategies. Weiss (1974) summarizes a wide body of opinion in the following way:

> In hospital, success in treating suicidal patients is more likely with a therapeutic regime having easy lines of communication than with the previously utilised strictures of rigid suicidal caution. Simply increasing the knowledge and sensitivity of all persons who are likely to come into contact with patients or with others who may be potentially suicidal has clearly proved of great importance both in therapy and prevention.

Consistent with this approach, Sainsbury (1963) has produced evidence to suggest that the open-door policy in mental hospitals has been associated with a considerable reduction in suicide rates among residents, despite increased admission rates for depressive psychosis and older patients.

The open psychiatric hospital system has now been with us for several decades and it is time to review whether its excellent principles have been fully vindicated. Although most practising clinicians support the open-door policy, slavish adherence to it may underemphasize the importance of physical security. When suicidal ideas are intense the only way to minimize the risk involved is to restrict the patient's liberty and to provide intensive surveillance. The practice of 'suicide caution' whereby a nurse was allocated to be with a suicidal patient at all times, often in a locked ward, has in general been discarded as inhuman and ineffective. Instead, we have built up an approach based on enlightened staff attitudes and communication in a situation where doors are not locked. The danger in the present system is that we may have followed new principles without due regard to the intrinsic value of the old. It can be extremely difficult in an open ward to provide adequate supervision of persons who are acutely suicidal. Many members of staff need to be involved and there are well-known danger periods, such as times of changeover from one nursing shift to another or at night. Even when staff numbers are adequate the possible misunderstandings between individuals are legion, especially when the patient deliberately misleads with regard to his intentions. Any open ward that admits suicidal patients should continually review whether it really can care for them adequately at all times of the day and night. Such a unit should have within it an area where observation can be maintained at a sufficient level of intensity, e.g. by suitable restriction of the number of exits and concentration of nursing staff. It should also have an agreed and explicit policy of management for patients of uncertain suicide risk. Whilst it is inappropriate to argue in favour of locked wards, there is much to be said for the concept of an intensive care area within the open ward system involving concentration of nursing staff as well as a degree of physical security. Unless these are available, the open system will force those in charge of management policy to take risks with inadequate supervision because of the limits of the care facility. Some suicides currently may well occur as a direct result of these deficiencies in the open ward system.

A set of policy rules is of course essential in any unit which cares for suicidal patients. These will to some extent be dictated by the general conditions which apply in any particular ward situation. Table 8 outlines one possible scheme for use in an open psychiatric ward. What is most important is that all persons concerned should understand the policy clearly. First and foremost, there should be adequate communication between the several members of the therapeutic team with an awareness of the various ways in which information sharing and surveillance may fail, a thorough understanding by all responsible staff members of the precise level of supervision agreed at any time, a general ethos that the patient can be effectively helped over a crisis, and a sense of trust between the various members of the therapeutic team itself.

The recurrent suicide risk

Some individuals at risk of suicide relapse fairly rapidly after initial intervention and present a pattern of recurrent suicidal crises. They often have a history of repeated hospital admissions with only very temporary or little change either in the way they feel or in their situation. Their management presents a particularly difficult problem.

Whilst some may appear to have mental illness which in itself is unresponsive to all available therapy, whether physical or psychotherapeutic, a high proportion of such individuals are locked in situational difficulties that appear to be intractable: these commonly take the form of unhappy marital relationships, social isolation, or chronic conflict. During the course of therapy intensive efforts must of course be made to achieve some resolution of situational difficulties, and in some cases

TABLE 8   Levels of supervision for suicidal patients

Level of special precaution	Details of supervision	Type of clinical problem
0	Normal ward routine, dressed, up and about.	Patient has settled into the ward, his problems have been assessed fully, and he is not regarded as being a suicidal risk (no suicidal ideation detected and behaviour consistent with this).
1 (minimal)	Not to leave the ward and to remain in pyjamas. Nurses advised to keep regular contact.	New admission after episode of self-harm. Not yet seen by ward doctor, denies suicidal ideas, and cleared by referring agency.
2 (moderate) personal nurse or intensive care area	Sufficient supervision to guarantee that the patient stays in the ward at all times. Observation is either continuous with special nurse or the patient is nursed in an intensive care area with restricted exits and frequent contact is maintained by staff at stipulated intervals, e.g. every 15–30 minutes.	Patients who though having active suicidal ideas are cooperative and open in their attitude and behaviour.
3 (intensive) personal nurse as well as intensive care area	Special nurse in attendance at all times, possibly nursed in bed. Adequate degree of physical security required (intensive care area in ward or locked ward, may need to be under observation or treatment order of relevant mental health legislative provision).	Active suicidal ideas. Threatens suicide or is unable to give guarantees about intentions. May have absconded from the open ward on one or more occasions, with or without episodes of self-harm. Behaviour unusual and suicide orientated.

neither the patient nor significant other persons in his life can contribute to any radical change. Though it is tempting to resort to some kind of forceful resolution of such difficulties, e.g. by threatening to break off therapy or by direct advice to separate from a difficult marital partner, this is not in general an acceptable strategy. We may well have to support such an individual over a prolonged period of time until some kind of improvement occurs either spontaneously or because the patient eventually marshalls enough personal resources himself. When we are involved in this kind of supportive therapy we should beware of the danger of producing an excessive degree of dependence on the part of the patient on the therapist, which may demonstrate itself by demands for increased frequency or longer appointments, or even admission to hospital. There is a need for a flexible approach, one which recognizes that whilst suicidal crises may arise in such intensity that hospital admission is indicated, it may nevertheless be necessary in many circumstances to tolerate a high degree of suicide risk whilst the patient remains in the community. An agreed contractual basis concerning frequency and duration of appointments may have to be applied rigidly. The whole situation calls for fine clinical judgement, in which the therapist neither underreacts nor overreacts to the recurrent crises but continues to make himself available in a clearly defined way. It is remarkable how effective even very brief interviews may be, perhaps lasting no more than twenty minutes every three or four weeks. Not infrequently confrontations arise in this kind of long-term support, particularly when the patient demands more intensive care than the therapist thinks appropriate. The therapist is by this time undoubtedly feeling frustrated at the failure of his efforts and he will be inclined to see the patient's talk of suicide as an unreasonable threat to control him. Impatience with an individual who gets depressed recurrently can cloud clinical judgement in such circumstances. Our own series of suicides illustrates these problems as they occurred in a psychiatric ward situation: half of our patients committed suicide after a confrontation with us in which they had insisted that they could not manage outside the hospital, though a decision was still made that they should do so. Such crises in treatment are not uncommon when an individual has become overdependent on hospital, and they are indeed necessary in some instances. On the other hand, quite clearly they can precipitate suicide if they misfire, especially when the therapist forces the issue in a unilateral way and the individuals concerned are tense, angry, and resentful about life-situation problems which have not been resolved.

Not infrequently, particularly difficult chronic problems find themselves passed from one agency to another in rapid succession, each one skilfully avoiding total responsibility for management. It is precisely in these situations that a suicidal person may accumulate many different helpers, reflecting the complexity of his social and medical problems. If the various agencies involved are too busy to meet or cannot elect to integrate their efforts, then the total help is likely to be fragmented, grossly inefficient, and even harmful.

The alcohol addict and suicide risk

The problems met in treating the alcoholic are of course the paradigm of those discussed in the previous section. He may have relapsed repeatedly, appearing to have failed to make use of help previously, he may present at times which seem grossly inconsiderate, and he may truly threaten suicide in what seems to be a superficial manipulative way, especially when he is drunk. In any event he is likely to alienate himself from our sympathy, and so our judgement regarding suicide risk may be impaired as a result. Indications of significant suicide risk in the chronic alcoholic include severe depressive symptoms, tension, and anger over situational difficulties which may have recently worsened, a history of deliberate drug overdosage in the recent past, and suicidal ideas which have been expressed consistently over a period of time, not merely when he was drunk.

Failed suicides

A small proportion of individuals who present with non-fatal deliberate self-harm have actually failed in a very determined attempt to end their lives. We will defer detailed consideration of this particular problem until later when it will be discussed in the context of non-fatal deliberate self-harm in general. At this point it is sufficient to note that one who has survived a serious attempt to end his own life may feel redoubled guilt at not having succeeded and he will tend to deny suicidal ideas. Hence it is important to look for inconsistencies between what he says, on the one hand, and his general behaviour, on the other, and to remember that the improvement in mood which may occur after an episode of self-harm may be short lasting. Someone who has taken a severe overdose or caused extensive self-laceration, having tried to avoid discovery and ensure success, who cannot reassure the interviewer about subsequent intent, has significant depressive symptoms, who would be returning to a worsened social situation or to social isolation, is male, middle aged or older, and has a chronic physical disease, would normally be regarded as being at high suicide risk and should preferably be treated in hospital, at least initially.

7

SUICIDE PREVENTION

From our discussion of the causes and manifest features of suicide few would conclude that this is entirely preventable: its origins are complex and they reside both in the individual and in his environment. The evidence does suggest, however, that we should be able to help many individuals in danger of suicide and effectively reduce the total number of deaths from this cause in any community. Suicide can justifiably be regarded as a major challenge in primary prevention. (W.H.O. 1974.).

We know that about half of the individuals who deliberately end their lives declare themselves as being in need of help by contacting medical services in the last few weeks of their lives. Yet although they make contact, they are not regularly recognized as being at risk of suicide. A considerable number show evidence of marked ambivalence about ending their lives and may well be open to influences which can help them to go on living. The most common psychological syndrome manifest at the time of suicide is depression: we know how variable that may be, how quickly it may respond to the correct form of treatment no matter how impossible the life situation, or how chronic the individual's psychological problems. Even the most vulnerable have a resilience which with help and time makes it possible for them to come back from the brink of despair and see a more positive side to existence. There is clearly enough evidence to give us confidence that suicide prevention may be both feasible and effective. We must therefore proceed to examine the ways in which a community might aim to reduce the incidence of suicide within its midst. We will be particularly concerned to define the most effective ways of making help available to those who need it and to look at those elements in our helping techniques which are most in need of refinement and development.

7.1 Making Contact with the Suicidal

A suicidal individual is more likely to declare his problems and actively turn for help if he thinks that a positive response will be obtained. Help which is offered must therefore appear relevant to the needs of those at risk, it should be such that persons in despair can see its value, and it should be readily available when needed.

Medical services

Undoubtedly many suicidal individuals make contact with established medical services either through their general practitioner or at a hospital. They may go to declare their true inner feelings in the hope that effective help will be forthcoming and they are most likely to do this when they are still ambivalent about killing themselves. They often make contact to present physical symptoms or to discuss specific psychological problems without declaring their suicidal feelings. The way they are received is therefore of crucial importance because if they are rejected or if the true nature of their difficulties is not appreciated then their resolve to end their lives is strengthened; even the experts are then seen to be unable to help. Skilled recognition of the suicidal and their various guises when they appear asking for help is therefore essential.

The matter is relatively easy when the patient is open and cooperative. The greatest obstacles occur when difficulties have been recurrent and intractible, often in the setting of social chaos: it is here that the doctor eventually so often loses heart and categorizes the patient as someone else's problem, irrelevant to medicine. Although he may be right in assuming that the social difficulties are paramount, his rejection can add the final seal to the patient's self-destructive despair. Such an approach, whereby a suicidal individual is assumed to be unamenable to help, ignores the fact that few if any are fully inaccessible, although many behave in an uncooperative way. Mere personal contact of limited therapeutic aim, e.g. by suggesting a further appointment, can itself be of immense value in a crisis situation. The distinction which we often make between medical and social problems is artificial, defensive, and unconstructive. Recognition of high-risk groups is of course important in helping us to suspect that suicidal feelings may be present, thereby facilitating individual clinical assessment.

In the United States of America the medical services have in many cities developed Suicide Prevention Centers. The first of these was established in Los Angeles in 1958 (Shneidman, Farberow, and Litman, 1961) and since then well over a hundred have proliferated. In general they have aimed at being part of the medical establishment, having close integration with health and welfare departments, as well as with police services and the local coroner's office. Apart from providing a special service for those patients who have been admitted to hospital after attempted suicide, people at risk in the community are encouraged to make direct crisis contact with the service. There has inevitably been much discussion regarding the effectiveness of this kind of approach to suicide prevention (Kiev, 1971, 1976), which assumes a degree of discrimination in the way persons in crisis will select a source of help, besides their willingness to turn to the established services. Kiev comments:

> There is no evidence to date that any of these centers which in the main specialise in telephone referral has reduced the suicide rate in the area they covered. Some have found only a small percentage, 15% in one report, of calls relate to suicide and that these are predominantly of low suicide risk. There are some who suggest that these centers be called crisis intervention centers since few of them provide treatment. (Kiev, 1971).

In response to such a commentary Litman and his colleagues calculated the suicide rates amongst the first thousand clients who had made contact with the Los Angeles Suicide Prevention Center during the period 1959–1962 and showed that they were greatly elevated compared with the general population in Los Angeles (Litman *et al.*, 1974). Suicide rates were greatest in the first six months but remained elevated during a six-year follow-up. In Los Angeles, 8 per cent. of certified suicides had been in contact with the Center at some time (Litman and Wold, 1976). Similar findings have been reported from the Cleveland Suicide Prevention Center (Sawyer, Sudak, and Hall, 1972) and the Chicago 'Call for Help' Clinic (Wilkins, 1970). Kiev's criticisms do not therefore appear to be fully justified, because quite clearly whatever preventive effects the centres may have had with regards to suicide deaths they did make contact with individuals at high risk for suicide—a necessary prerequisite if we are to help them. The fact that people with other kinds of problem also made contact seems hardly relevant. Nor should we use suicide statistics as the only criterion against which to judge the efficacy of such centres, because we do not know what the suicide rate would be in their absence. This is not to deny that their efficacy should be evaluated, but merely to emphasize the need to use relevant criteria in doing so: they may eventually be found to have many other kinds of benefit, e.g. by reducing morbidity from the secondary effects of non-fatal drug overdosage or self-injury, or they may delay suicide deaths and improve the quality of life for clients and relatives before suicide occurs. Kiev may well be correct, however, in his assertion that crisis invervention will eventually prove to be a more accurate description of the most important role of the centres. Their value in maintaining contact with vulnerable individuals long after a crisis has, however, also been rightly emphasized (Litman and Wold, 1976).

In Great Britain the medical and psychiatric services have not developed specialized suicide prevention centres along the lines of the American model, but have concentrated much more on working in parallel with and supporting voluntary agencies based in the community.

Voluntary agencies

The different style of suicide prevention which has arisen in Great Britain when compared with the United States is of course of great interest. Whilst no special provision for suicide prevention has developed within the framework of the National Health Service, nor in the statutory agencies such as the Social and Probation Services for that matter, though this is not meant in any way to disregard their work in this field, the community itself has been extremely active through the organization known as The Samaritans founded by the Rev. Chad Varah in 1953. People in despair are encouraged to make contact, through a telephone service which is actively publicized; the help, which is termed 'befriending', is offered without obligation by ordinary people who refuse to be partisan in any way, whether religious, political, medical, or otherwise. The great majority of professionals, whether they be psychiatrists, general practitioners, or social workers, give the Samaritan organization their wholehearted support, providing complementary back-up where necessary. They view its independence with approval because they recognize that the organization has a different role than their own: its strength resides in the fact that it originates in the community itself. There are of course other organizations such as the Marriage Guidance Council and also various agencies aimed at students and adolescents, which make major contributions to helping the suicidal individual. They certainly make contact with clients at risk, particularly with those who would hesitate to use a telephone call-in service or the more traditional medical facilities. Help is thus offered to the potential suicide by seeking out those in despair, as in the case of the Samaritans, or is aimed at specific personal problems such as those concerning marriage, sex, or adolescence.

Again it has been asked whether the Samaritan organization really does attract persons who are at increased risk of suicide as opposed to those who have trivial problems. There is now very good evidence that it does: those clients who default have been shown to have a suicide rate thirty to forty times the expected during the following year, particularly in the month after contact is lost (Barraclough and Shea, 1970).

Contact with the community

When a suicidal individual is in that tug-of-war state of indecision as to whether he really will kill himself, his readiness to turn for help to those around him, whether they be relatives, friends, work colleagues, or neighbours, will depend upon their attitudes both towards him and to such issues as suicide, deviant behaviour, and psychological problems. Willingness to discuss feelings in an unprejudiced way is an important element here though the barriers and taboos which exist in normal social and family relationships are enormous; hence the frequent need for anonymity in the professional setting or through a voluntary agency such as the Samaritans. We know that suicide itself has always been the subject of superstition, anxiety, and many misconceptions. The facts of suicide should be included in the basic health and hygiene teaching at every school so that each young adult will be furnished with reliable information on which to base his own reaction when he encounters someone who is in despair or indeed if he should need help himself. There is no evidence that such basic education does anything other than good.

7.2 Providing Effective Help

Closely related to the suicidal person's willingness to make contact is the type of help which he will receive whenever he does so. What happens to him will vary depending on whether he chooses to make contact with a medical or voluntary agency, although ideally there will be close integration between the two.

Medical services

In Great Britain medical help is sought by a considerable proportion of suicidal persons in the weeks before their death: in their recent study of 100 suicides, Barraclough *et al.* (1974) found that two-thirds had visited their family doctor in the month before their death 40 per cent. in the previous week. One-quarter were also seeing a psychiatrist, and in many others no doubt the treatment had been influenced by previous psychiatric advice. Most of the patients were recognized as having psychological disturbance, 80 per cent. receiving psychotropic drugs, although some irregularities occurred in the way these were used. Antidepressants were often given in low, possibly ineffective doses, sometimes over long periods without obvious improvement, and barbiturates, phenothiazines, and monor tranquillizers were probably overprescribed.

Over half of all suicides are probably under medical or psychiatric treatment at the time they kill themselves and are receiving some kind of psychotropic drug treatment. Those who see mental illness as the main cause of suicide and who rely on psychotropic medication in its treatment will wish to scrutinize the drug regimes in such cases in order to improve their efficacy, perhaps advocating larger doses and greater discrimination in the way they are used in the treatment of specific syndromes. Others will question the value of such drugs, especially in persons whose problems are primarily related to personality difficulties and social problems, and in whom psychological disturbance such as severe depression is clearly a secondary end result. Traditionally the psychotropic drugs have been evaluated in terms of the response of symptoms to them. There is little information with regards to the social settings in which they are used. Are they just as useful in a young woman whose husband has left her to bring up a baby in a tenement room with no hot water as in a middle class married woman with no situational difficulties? In what setting are they particularly liable to be misused through deliberate self-overdosage? What kind of personal support and psychotherapy is essential in parallel with their use, how often, and by whom? Such facts about the setting in which these drugs are used are just as important as their dosage. Whether ease of access to drugs and their general availability really affects the incidence of suicide is not yet clear, but the relevance of these issues to impulsive acts of self-poisoning is undeniable.

Certain aspects of the psychiatric services themselves need clarification with regards to suicide prevention. The role of hospitalization in the care of severe depression has been challenged, particularly when it is enforced on the patient. There is considerable emotive reaction against treatment such as electroplexy, so much so that its objective evaluation may be made more difficult. We still need to know more about nursing techniques for those patients who present very high suicide risks, particularly with regards to the value of intensive surveillance and restricted freedom of movement. Clearer understanding is also needed to help us decide on the exact mix between physical treatment, on the one hand, and psychological ones, on the other. The high proportion (30 per cent.) of depressive suicides which was found by Pokorny (1960, 1964) during the first few months after discharge from psychiatric hospital is disturbing. These findings may of course be interpreted in various ways, but it does emphasize the need for continued intensive support when an individual returns to the community from psychiatric hospital.

The use of predictive scales in the detection of individuals who are at high risk of suicide has been the focus of a great deal of attention in recent years and although progress has so far been limited certain important conclusions are now clear. Litman and his colleagues at the Los Angeles Suicide Prevention Center consider that suicide is too complex to be encompassed by one predictive scale and the data to be included will probably need to vary from one community to another. Factors which predict acute risk of suicide may be different from those which are relevant to risk over an extended period (Litman *et al.*, 1974). Most predictive scales incorporate both clinical and demographic data. Diggory (1974) has pointed out the low level of significance which demographic data may have in an individual case, reflecting the great degree of individual variability in the circumstances of suicide. To illustrate his point Diggory quotes data from an earlier study by Tuckman and Youngman (1963a, 1963b) in which 7 per cent. of the sample of white males over 45 years of age, living alone, and having made a suicide attempt, killed themselves within a year after the attempt. If this criterion was used in a predictive scale it would be necessary to allow for the fact that it would be wrong in 93 per cent. of cases.

Lester (1974) also reminds us that even amongst high-risk groups, suicide is a rare event, and prediction of a rare event is extremely difficult. The correct balance between clinical assessment with its intuitive holistic judgements and the use of demographic data rests upon a proper understanding of the differences between these two kinds of information. Clinical data can be more easily tailored to the individual and is perhaps more relevant to short-term prediction, whereas demographic facts are more useful with regards to the long term, as well as in planning the location of services in areas where high-risk individuals are concentrated. Even when apparently simple variables such as suicidal intent (Beck, Schuyler, and Herman, 1974) have been used in devising prediction scales their heterogeneous and complex nature has become clear. We may conclude in the light of their difficulties that prediction scales must always be used with caution and in parallel with careful direct assessment of the individual concerned with full knowledge of his particular life situation.

Voluntary agencies

We have already seen that a voluntary initiative such as the Samaritan organization does attract to it a considerable number of clients who are at high suicide risk. But does it help to prevent people from killing themselves? Bagley (1968) compared the average suicide rates in fifteen towns in England and Wales (all those in which a Samaritan service had been operational in 1964 for at least two years) with those in control towns, matched for major population and social class characteristics. It was concluded that Samaritan services had been associated with a relative decline in suicide risk in the towns where they had operated. The association could not be claimed as causal since for any town the same underlying social factors might have been responsible both for the setting up of the Samaritan scheme and for a subsequent reduction in the suicide rate. More recent studies, using different and more sophisticated methods of choosing control towns, have failed to confirm Bagley's findings (Barraclough, Jennings, and Moss, 1977; Jennings, Barraclough, and Moss, 1978). One major investigational problem has been to control for the undoubted impact on the suicide rate achieved by the change from coal gas to the less toxic natural gas for domestic use in the United Kingdom. In the early 1960s, about one-third of all suicides in England and Wales were due to coal gas poisoning; this proportion subsequently fell progressively until in recent years it has been practically zero. The change to natural gas for domestic use in the United Kingdom is now complete, and comparison of suicide rates in various cities should in future be less complicated. However, this will still remain a complex area of investigation, and we need more sophisticated criteria than official suicide statistics if the evaluation of suicide prevention agencies is to be adequately carried out (Lancet, 1978).

In 1976 the Samaritans had 150 centres in Great Britain with overseas branches in nine other countries, the first American branch having opened in Boston in 1973 (Fox, 1976; Varah, 1973). Whatever may be the difficulties in evaluating this organization in terms of its prevention of suicide, we must agree that it embodies sound fundamental principles in helping those in despair: it reaches out to encourage them to make contact, it harnesses human volunteer potential from within the community itself, it is non-partisan, and it fosters an attitude of unreserved acceptance towards any individual, whoever he may be or whatever he may have done. Initial telephone contact is often followed up by direct personal contact both in crisis and in the form of support over a considerable period of time. Autonomous organizations such as these deserve our fullest support.

Society at large

Much of our discussion concerning suicide and its prevention has been concerned with those factors which are either personal, reflecting some kind of psychological or physical vulnerability, or situational stresses relevant to an individual's day-to-day life. At this stage it is also necessary for us to note certain features of modern life, particularly in certain areas of large cities, which may constitute pervasive forces acting on the individual in an adverse way. Maris (1971) has attempted to delineate such elements of urban living, commenting that the contemporary city dweller usually does not behave socially out of concern for others so much as out of fear of negative legal sanctions, or discontinuance of services provided by them. This situation has arisen out of an increasing division of labour, with the result that our survival is increasingly contingent upon more people who provide needed goods and services. In the setting of increasing population density, escalation of crime rates, and polarization between ethnic groups, people are forced to live in close proximity yet they interact on a depersonalized professional basis rather than spontaneously and diffusely: a kind of rampant solipsism exists under the guise of 'doing your own thing'. A vulnerable individual may find himself isolated and alienated in a fragmented, divided, and avaricious society. We need to take these comments seriously. Our efforts to prevent suicide by increasing the availability and effectiveness of services will have trivial benefit if those at risk are for the majority of their day-to-day existence subject to relentless adverse social influences.

7.3 Prevention of Suicide at all Costs?

A certain number of suicides will always occur without previous contact with preventive agencies and in the absence of warning signs to others. A number of these will be regarded as rational and perhaps justifiable, such as when an individual has always wanted to cheat old age by organizing his own death, thereby retaining some control over it by making it predictable, or when someone sacrifices himself in an altruistic way in order to benefit the welfare of others. We cannot comment profitably further on these examples of suicide because they reflect individual moral and religious beliefs which are of course extremely varied. On the other hand, certain problems of suicide prevention present us with very real dilemmas. What should our attitudes be to the elderly and isolated who feel that life is spent, or to those who have a painful terminal disease when they indicate that they wish to die? How vigorously should we try to prevent suicide in such individuals?

There is clearly a considerable present-day interest in 'rational' suicide, as to whether it occurs at all and if it does with what frequency. This of course reflects a preoccupation with freedom of the individual and his protection from intrusion by others into the privacy of his personal life.

When faced with someone who asks to be allowed to commit suicide without hindrance, there is rarely enough evidence to indicate that we should stand aside and let it happen: it is my personal view that for all practical purposes such a policy is never advisable.

Such an uncompromising approach is necessary because of the uncertainty and fallibility of the evidence on which we have to base our decisions. Suicidal individuals test us out, ask to be relieved of the need to continue seeing us, whilst at the same time expressing relief at being able to do so, and challenge us to declare the situation as hopeless. Nobody views death without ambivalence. Although persons in despair see their situation as impossible, such an attitude often changes in the course of time through a resilience and adaptability to adversity which may be found even in the most vulnerable. The isolated elderly certainly present us with a particular ethical and moral challenge, concerning not so much whether they should be allowed to take their own lives if they wish but rather why we have allowed them to become isolated and despairing in the first place. All these are adequate reasons why we cannot connive with suicide: to do so would be to assume an unjustifiable omnipotence of attitude in the face of many uncertainties and to deny the wish to live, which is perhaps the strongest of all man's instincts and which is never fully extinguished while he continues to exist.

Part II

NON-FATAL DELIBERATE SELF-HARM

8

INCIDENCE AND METHODS

In order to discuss non-fatal episodes of self-harm as distinct from suicide we need from the outset to reach an agreed definition of the problem involved.

8.1 Case Definition

Stengel (1952) was one of the first to emphasize the many differences between persons who kill themselves and those who harm themselves sublethally. He considered, however, that demonstrable conscious intent of self-destruction was an essential component in both groups, implying that those who survive are in fact failed suicides. Hence he suggested the terms 'suicide' and 'attempted suicide', elaborating this approach to the problem in a classic monograph (Stengel and Cook, 1958).

Since then it has become clear that such a rigorous case definition of non-fatal self-harm poses major difficulties, because as we will see many non-fatal episodes do not appear to be related at the time to conscious ideas of suicide, at least not ones which can be demonstrated by subsequent review. It also seems inappropriate to accord motivation such a key place in case definition in view of the major difficulties in assessing it in a reliable and objective way.

Current definitions of non-fatal acts of self-harm concentrate on their deliberate and conscious character, whether or not the wish to achieve self-destruction can be demonstrated. Some examples will serve to illustrate this point. Kreitman (1977) and his colleagues in Edinburgh use the following case definition: '. . . a non fatal act in which an individual deliberately causes self injury or ingests a substance in excess of any prescribed or generally recognised therapeutic dose'. This is similar to that used by Bancroft and this Oxford group (Bancroft et al., 1975): 'Self poisoning is defined as the intentional self administration of more than the prescribed dose of any drug, whether or not there was evidence that the act was intended to cause self harm. Self injury includes those episodes recognised as deliberate.'

Our Bristol studies were based on the following case definition: '. . . a deliberate non fatal act, whether physical, drug overdosage or poisoning, done in the knowledge that it was potentially harmful, and in the case of drug overdosage, that the amount taken was excessive'.

Certain problems occur in applying this type of case definition. It is not always easy to distinguish between accidental and deliberate episodes, and occasionally it is necessary to depend upon other evidence than the patient's version, if necessary countermanding his own account of events and intention. Alcohol intoxication is excluded unless it is accompanied by other types of self-poisoning or self-injury. Drug addicts who have used addictive agents for 'kicks' are only included if it can be demonstrated that self-harm was deliberate and intentional. In London as many as 14 per cent. of self-poisonings seen in Accident Departments occur during the course of drug addiction (Ghodse, 1976). The use of non-ingestants or poisons usually presents fewer problems with regards to intent, though even here accidental intake is occasionally difficult to exclude. The definition does not encompass threats of self-harm, though here again problems of case definition can arise; certain instances when exposure to serious risk has occurred, e.g. by hanging off cliffs or high buildings, might be included.

Non-fatal episodes of self-harm may be referred to collectively as problems of self-poisoning and self-injury. The Edinburgh school has suggested that a single term 'parasuicide' is appropriate because it 'refers to a behavioural analogue of suicide but without considering a psychological orientation towards death being in any way essential to the definition'. Yet it also serves to emphasize that the two forms of behaviour are closely associated (Kreitman, 1977). We have used the term 'non-fatal deliberate self-harm' as perhaps more appropriate a way of describing a form of behaviour which besides including failed suicides embraces many episodes in which actual self-destruction was clearly not intended. The general meaning of self-harm is also well suited to cover the wide variety of methods used, including drug overdosage, self-poisoning with non-ingestants, the use of other chemicals such as gases, as well as laceration and other forms of physical injury. In our subsequent discussions, for the sake of brevity, all acute non-fatal acts of deliberate self-harm will be referred to as DSH, thereby distinguishing them from suicide.

8.2 Incidence of DSH

Wherever surveys have been conducted the problem of DSH has been found to have increased progressively in Western countries since the early 1960s. Weissman (1974) and Wexler, Weissman, and Kasl (1978) have reviewed the literature for the period 1960–1975 demonstrating a consistent pattern of individual and demographic characteristics as well as the methods used. In order to illustrate our discussions we will also refer in particular detail to several British studies, especially those in which case detection seems to have been most complete.

The earliest studies from Edinburgh and Sheffield provided data for the period 1960–1964 and since then the situation has been monitored in several cities throughout Britain. Some reports have concerned themselves with hospital admission statistics: in Sheffield (Smith, 1972) there was an increase of 100 per cent. in medical admissions for self-poisoning during the period 1960–1971 and in Newcastle Upon Tyne (Smith and Davidson, 1971) an overall increase of 77 per cent. in hospital admissions for 'attempted suicide' occurred during the period between 1962–1964 and 1966–1969. Similar findings were reported from Cardiff (Graham and Hitchens, 1967) and Oxford (Evans, 1967) for the period 1960–1965.

The Regional Poisoning Treatment Centre in Edinburgh has provided the most thorough documentation over the longest period. Detailed statistics have been available in Edinburgh each year since 1967, providing valuable reference data concerning trends in the incidence and other characteristics of DSH (Holding et al., 1977). The Oxford and Bristol studies have also aimed at thorough case detection by including accident and emergency referrals as well as hospital admissions statistics: in Oxford, general practitioners were also encouraged to report cases directly to the research team. As a result a comprehensive and very valuable and reliable picture of DSH became available in these three cities during the early 1970s and their detailed comparison became possible because age specific rates and other data were recorded in standardized form. Before proceeding further we need to be satisfied with regards to the reliability of such hospital-based statistics. It could be that a significant proportion of cases are treated by general practitioners without referral to hospital and such patients might differ significantly from those who are referred for more intensive treatment. The Edinburgh workers investigated this aspect of the problem thoroughly using a telephone call-in system for general practitioners and they concluded that their results underestimated the total size of the problem by at least 30 per cent., and when all episodes were considered there were significant qualitative

90

differences between the general practitioner-treated cases and those going to hospital (Kennedy and Kreitman, 1973; Kreitman, 1977). Hospital-based studies cannot therefore be assumed to be fully representative of the total DSH problem in the community.

The crude male and female DSH rates in Edinburgh, Oxford, and Bristol based on hospital statistics during the period 1962–1967 are shown in Figure 5. It is seen that rates in females consistently exceed those in males and for each study there has been a progressive rise in DSH incidence during the whole of the period. In Edinburgh the problem has increased by 10 per cent. per annum and rates have been consistently

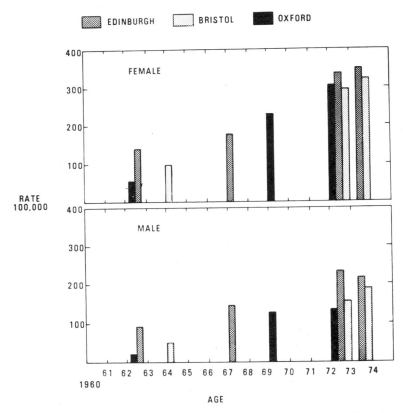

FIGURE 5. Trends in incidence of non-fatal deliberate self harm 1962–74. (Persons admitted to hospital. Rates per 100,000 total population over 15 years of age.) (Evans, 1967; Aitken *et al.*, 1969, Roberts and Hoopes, 1969; Bancroft *et al.*, 1975; Morgan *et al.*, 1975a; Holding *et al.*, 1977)

higher than in Oxford and Bristol. The rate of increase in these two cities seems to have been greater than in Edinburgh, however, and there has been a tendency for the DSH rates in all three cities to approximate in the more recent years. It is possible that this reflects variations in the efficiency of case detection rather than true differences in trends between the three cities: early studies in Oxford and Bristol relied heavily on indirect assessment based on hospital admission records whereas the Poisoning Treatment Centre at Edinburgh has consistently been highly effective in case detection throughout the whole period.

Age and sex

It is generally agreed that the highest rates occur in young adults, and at all ages except in the elderly rates in females exceed those in males. The female/male overall ratio in published studies has usually been within the range 1.4 to 2.2/1. Exceptions are found in Malmo, Sweden, and Boston, United States, where an equal distribution between the two sexes has been reported. In Traralgon, Victoria, Australia, and Yukon, Canada, females are reported to exceed males by 3 to 4/1 (Wexler, Weissman, and Kasl, 1978). The age specific rates for DSH episodes in Bristol (Morgan, Pocock, and Pottle, 1975) are illustrated in Figure 6, and in their general characteristics these are typical findings. In such a situation where marked variation in incidence occurs with age it is obviously most

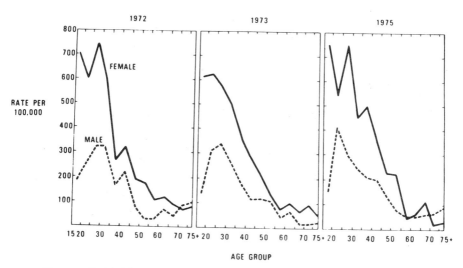

FIGURE 6. Deliberate self harm inception rates: Bristol County Borough, 1972, 1973 and 1975. (Morgan, Pocock, and Pottle, 1975)

important to refer to age specific rates when discussing trends, and comparison of crude overall rates is far less useful. Peak incidence occurs between 20 and 30 years in men, although in Edinburgh the 15 to 20 age group in 1974 also showed a very high rate. In women the highest rates occur between 15 and 30 years, although a high incidence in the 15 to 20 age group has been a striking feature of the DSH problem in more recent years. The high rates in this female age group in Bristol are particularly striking.

Between the 1962–1975 period the greatest increase in incidence has occurred in adolescents and young adults. Thus in Bristol the rates in the age group of 15 to 20 years increased 18 times for women and 4.5 times for men. These contrast with the rates in older patients: for males over 55 years they barely changed, though in females over 50 years they doubled.

The trends demonstrated in Figure 5 suggest that between 1972–1975 the rate of increase in incidence tended to level off as if the so-called epidemic of self-harm was beginning to reach its zenith. In Edinburgh male rates fell in 1973–1974 whilst those in females increased less than in previous years (Holding *et al.*, 1977). Only time will tell whether these falls will continue.

The findings from Oxford suggest that the rate of increase may also be lessening, but there is so far no indication of this in Bristol. That there is no reason for optimism with regards to the general incidence of DSH is supported by two other kinds of evidence. The Edinburgh team has produced data concerning 'first-ever' DSH which reveals that the greatest increase in this type of DSH has occurred in young females aged 15 to 19 years and in males aged 25 to 34 years. The pattern of the future will depend upon whether this form of behaviour, once adopted, is continued with increasing age. Further, using national hospital statistics on self-poisoning, Alderson (1974) has carried out a patient cohort analysis which showed a 'horrific' rise in incidence in each succeeding age group with no evidence of an age peak in early adult life. Clearly there is little evidence for optimism that in general the so-called DSH epidemic is abating.

8.3 Methods of DSH

In recent years the great majority of patients who make contact with hospital after non-fatal episodes of deliberate self-harm have taken a drug overdose. Table 9 illustrates the relevant findings in the Bristol area (Morgan, Pocock, and Pottle, 1975). Only a small proportion used non-ingested poisoning, gassing, or laceration; the overwhelming pre-

TABLE 9   Deliberate self-harm: breakdown of methods used (persons attending Accident and Emergency Departments, City of Bristol, 1972 and 1973)

Method	Number of patients	Percentage
Self-poisoning		
Drug overdose	1,440	91.8
Non-ingestant	7	0.5
Gassing	8	0.5
Laceration	76	4.8
Other (immersion,		
hanging, jumping)	16	1.1
Drug overdose and		
any other	22	1.3
Total	1,569	100

ponderance of drug overdose (93.1 per cent.) was quite clear.

Analysis of the type of drugs involved (Figure 7) showed that psychotropic drugs, tranquillizers, antidepressants, and non-barbiturate hypnotics were used in 49 per cent. Much less commonly the overdose consisted of barbiturates (14 per cent.) or salicylates (17 per cent.). In addition a small number used a wide variety of prescribed compounds such as antibiotics, steroids, antispasmodics, or hormone preparations. The tendency by some to use more than one type of drug and the difficulty in identifying the precise agent involved can at times complicate the problem of physical resuscitation. A more recent survey of patients attending London Accident Departments suggests that nearly 50 per cent. of DSH episodes involve more than one drug (Ghodse, 1976). Most drugs used originate from medical prescription: in Bristol 78 per cent. of patients used prescribed drugs, 67 per cent. their own and 11 per cent. drugs meant for someone else.

The drugs chosen for overdose differ significantly between the various age groups. Our Bristol study has shown that use of hypnotics including barbiturates increases with age (taken by 58 per cent. of patients aged 55 years and over) (Figure 8). Analgesics including salicylates, and which of course are far less likely to have originated from medical prescription, were more commonly used by younger patients (76 per cent. of those aged 15 to 19 years) Tranquillizers constituted the main drug group in patients aged 20 to 34 years.

A very striking feature of DSH is the fact that the majority reach hospital and survive; in fact only in a small minority is there a serious threat to life. In Bristol it was found that 26 per cent. of men and 15 per cent. of women were at some point unconscious for more than twelve hours and 4 per cent. needed admission to the intensive care unit. However, in the great majority only simple nursing care was required. At this point we may also note that only a minority appear to have had conscious expectations of dying or actually had wanted to die. Well over half (68 per cent.) warned others before or soon after the event and only 27 per cent. tried to avoid discovery. These points will be discussed later when motivation is dealt with in more detail.

These findings are with only minor variation typical of those reported elsewhere (Holding *et al.*, 1977; Weissman, 1974). Weissman comments that the drugs used in each country bear a general relationship to those which are most widely prescribed and available. The changing pattern of agents used in DSH has been most fully documented in Edinburgh. When Kessel carried out his survey there in the early 1960s he noted that in the

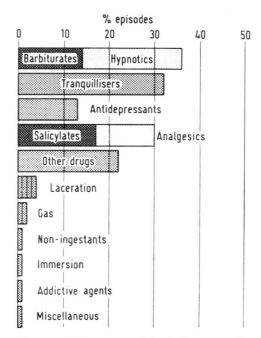

FIGURE 7. Agents used in deliberate self harm. (368 interviewed patients) (Morgan, Burns-Cox, Pocock, and Pottle, 1975)

1930s the majority of admissions for DSH, though small in total compared with those of today, were due to non-drug poisons, mainly lysol and other corrosive agents, and coal gas. These have now of course become uncommon. Barbiturates increased in importance as a cause of DSH in the 1950s and these were regarded by Kessell in 1965 as an 'outstanding problem'. They have, however, become progressively less common in the last decade, to be replaced by the rapid rise in the use of prescribed tranquillizers and non-barbiturate hypnotics in DSH. These issues will also be discussed later in more detail.

The use of salicylates and other analgesics is worthy of particular note for several reasons: not only do they occur in more than 20 per cent. of episodes of DSH but their ease of availability without prescription over the counter, their preferential use by teenagers, and the dangerous toxicity of drugs such as aspirin and paracetamol, even in moderate

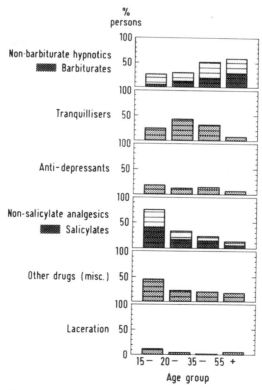

FIGURE 8. Principle methods in deliberate self harm. (By age groups) (Morgan, Burns-Cox, Pocock, and Pottle, 1975)

overdosage, all emphasize that this is a serious aspect of the DSH problem.

No discussion of the methods used in DSH would be complete without reference to the role played by alcohol. This will also be discussed in more detail when we come to consider concomitants and causes of DSH, but at this stage we should note that recent alcohol intake (within the previous six hours) was found in our Bristol study to have occurred in more than half of the men and a quarter of the women. In Edinburgh considerably higher figures were reported for 1974—two-thirds of male and 45 per cent. of female admissions having consumed alcohol shortly before the episode of DSH, the proportion of women having increased considerably in recent years (Holding et al., 1977).

Self injury

Only a small proportion of those who attend hospital because of DSH have resorted to physical injury, usually in the form of self-laceration. The true incidence of this in the general population is difficult to estimate. A survey in St. Louis based on reports concerning 'attempted suicide' from many kinds of community agencies and hospitals (Clendenin and Murphy, 1971) revealed that 11.5 per cent. had cut themselves: of these 85 per cent. had cut their wrists, the remainder having inflicted lacerations on some other part of the body. A very small number, about 1 per cent., lacerated themselves having also taken a drug overdose. Our Bristol findings concerning episodes of DSH reaching Hospital Accident and Emergency Departments from a population of approximately half a million revealed that 6 per cent. involved self-laceration, most commonly affecting one or both wrists. More men than women attended hospital because of self-laceration. It is also noteworthy that out of more than 1,500 persons attending hospital because of DSH in a two-year period, only one involved physical injury due to a firearm and one due to self-inflicted burns.

Self-laceration may be further classified according to the extent and character of the injury (Ping Nie Pao, 1969). A small number, frequently males, and usually very depressed and suicidal, inflict a single deep coarse incision which is close to a vital point and which endangers life. The majority, more often female, resort to delicate superficial and carefully designed incisions which usually heal without scarring. Such superficial laceration is more likely to be repetitive though it is less commonly associated with overt depression and despair. Self-laceration is discussed in more detail in Chapter 10.

8.4 Suicide and Non-Fatal Deliberate Self-Harm

Our discussions so far have demonstrated several major differences between the problem of suicide, on the one hand, and non-fatal deliberate self-harm (DSH), on the other. We will later discover others but at this point we may list those dealt with so far:

(1) The explosive increase in the incidence of DSH since the 1960s contrasts sharply with the tendency for overall suicide rates to fall.

(2) Suicide increases in incidence progressively with age whereas the greatest incidence of DSH is in young adults.

(3) In all age groups male rates of suicide exceed those in females whilst the opposite applies to rates for DSH, except in the very elderly.

(4) Although poisoning by drugs is a major cause of both suicide and DSH, its massive preponderance as the main cause of the latter contrasts with suicide, in which various forms of physical violence are relatively more common.

(5) Although the incidence of suicide some time after DSH is increased, it is nevertheless small, an overall 1 per cent. (approximately) committing suicide the subsequent year. Only a minority have conscious ideas of suicide at the time of DSH.

Any attempt to compare the incidence of suicide and DSH is somewhat meaningless unless the marked rate differentials between various age groups are taken into account. Table 10 illustrates this by using data from Bristol during the period 1968–1973. In the elderly, rates for DSH exceed those for suicide by the modest factor of 2 in males and 6 in females. In young adults, however, a dramatic difference between the size of the two problems is seen in the two sexes. In females aged 15 to 24 years the rates for DSH exceed those for suicide by a factor of 400, whilst in males the factor is 20.

98

TABLE 10 Comparison between age specific rates of suicide and non-fatal deliberate self-harm (DSH) in Bristol (1968–1973)

Age group	Males					Females				
	15–24	25–34	35–44	45–64	65+	15–24	25–34	35–44	45–64	65+
Suicide rate (average 1968–1973)	10	12	16	10	32	1.5	9.5	9	16	13
DSH rate (1972)	200	300	170	20	60	600	700	300	200	80
Ratio of DSH suicide	20	25	11	2	2	400	74	33	13	6

9

CORRELATES

Before we can proceed to consider the possible causes of the massive increase in non-fatal deliberate self-harm which has occurred in recent years we need to examine factors which may have causal significance both in the individual and with regards to his situation. These will be dealt with in two stages. First, we will be concerned with those psychological and environmental factors which may be termed predisposing and which have extended back for some considerable time. Second, we will examine factors which are more recent in onset and so are concomitant with DSH itself.

9.1 Predisposition

Situational and personal factors

There are two ways in which the social background of the DSH problem may be studied. The most common and direct method is by way of information obtained from interview with a series of patients after episodes of DSH: in parallel with this the ecological approach looks at the distribution of cases throughout the community. Our Bristol findings demonstrated that each method may facilitate the other.

Bristol forms a discrete urban area with a population of just over half a million. It is surrounded by relatively sparsely populated rural areas and it borders on the Bristol Channel (Figure 9). The city itself shows marked social zoning. The poorest and most overcrowded residential part is found centrally in the St. Pauls and City Road areas. Most of the nineteenth century artisan residential areas are to the east and south of the centre, having been built in proximity to the latter-day coalfields in Keynsham and Bedminster. The best-quality residential area is mainly on the north-west side of Clifton. Private and council house estates are also found in the newer residential areas, especially in the outer northern and southern suburbs.

During 1972 and 1973 the DSH problem in the whole of the Bristol area was evaluated by means of a case register: it was possible to detect all patients who attended any local Accident and Emergency Department or who were admitted to any of the three general hospitals in the area during that time. It was then possible to calculate inception rates for each electoral ward using data from the 1971 National Census. A very strongly centripetal distribution of DSH throughout the city was demonstrated in both 1972 and 1973. A similar though less striking pattern was found in a later survey in 1975 (Figure 10). The highest rates of DSH occur both centrally and in the council housing estates to the north and south. In view of the age-related nature of DSH incidence it was necessary to allow for differences in age structure of the various ward populations. Age

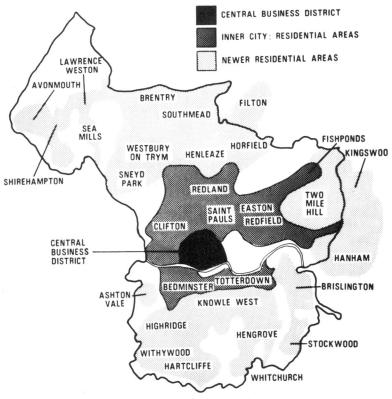

FIGURE 9. Bristol residential areas

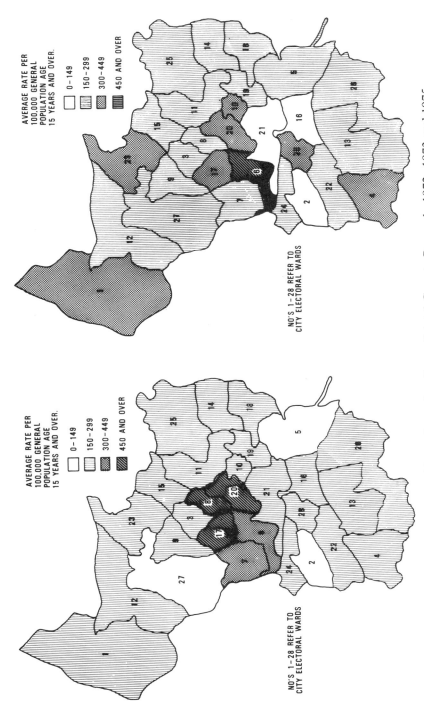

FIGURE 10. Deliberate self harm inception Rates Bristol County Borough, 1972–1973 and 1975

specific DSH rates were therefore utilized in comparing the different electoral wards, using the 15 to 39 year age group which showed the highest incidence rates. In this way it was possible to show that DSH incidence for persons aged 15 to 39 years living in certain central areas (wards 8, 17, and 20) were 1.6 to 2.8 times greater than the city average. In the St. Pauls area (ward 20) 1.6 per cent. of females in this age group showed some form of DSH each year. The centripetal pattern was highly significant statistically and there seemed no reason to believe that it reflected differential availability of hospital services throughout the city. It was not possible to be certain, however, of the extent to which it was explicable in terms of a greater population mobility which seemed likely in the central areas. This would of course increase the population at risk there, rendering ward populations estimates based on a single population count too low, thereby leading to artificially inflated DSH rates.

Using social data from the National Census it was possible to demonstrate the clear relationship between the incidence of DSH and social conditions. The inner city high-rate areas around St. Paul's were those of substandard housing, overcrowding, and with poor amenities; nearly 20 per cent. of their population were born outside the United Kingdom; they contain one-third of all Bristol's new commonwealth immigrants and a high proportion of unskilled manual labourers. In contrast the western part of the high-rate central area contained a large number of students and young professionals and a high proportion of rented accommodation. The contrast between the central areas and those of lowest DSH inception rates (wards 5 and 27) is very striking. In the latter there is a high proportion of owner-occupied households with many more professionals, employers, and managers (ward 27) and manual workers (ward 5). The age specific rates for DSH in these high- and low-rate wards differed by up to a factor of 8 for females and 6 for males. Distribution of DSH was correlated with various social indices available through the National Census (Table 11) and the findings suggested that overcrowding, lack of domestic amenities, and proportion of immigrants were important concomitant factors. No such relationship

. TABLE 11   Socioeconomic correlates of deliberate self-harm (Spearman rank correlation coefficient)

Year	Overcrowding	Lack of amenities	Proportion of immigrants	Lack of car
1972–1973	0.76 (<0.01)	0.45 (<0.01)	0.60 (<0.01)	0.49 (<0.01)
1975	0.69 (<0.01)	0.41 (<0.05)	0.69 (<0.01)	0.37 (<0.05)

was found with reference to the proportion in each ward of one-person households, council housing, or privately rented accommodation.

The precise meaning of these results can only be determined in the light of information obtained directly from the patient interviews. These were in fact carried out in a series of 368 patients admitted to one of the Bristol hospitals following DSH in 1972; the relevant findings are shown in Table 12.

TABLE 12   Socioeconomic characteristics of 368 patients interviewed after deliberate self-harm (figures indicate percentage of patients in study; city average, where available, is in brackets)

Social class	I	1.6	(4)
	II	10.1	(13)
	III	48.6	(52)
	IV	22.3	(18)
	V	14.1	(10)
Ethnic group	European		97.8 (97)
	Indo—Pakistani		0.8 (0.6)
	West Indian		1.4 (1)
At present address less than one year	40.6		
Overcrowded accommodation (< 1.5) persons per room	6.8 (1.3)		
Living alone	10.1 (8.4 for persons below pensionable age)		
Previously in prison	7.6		
Child of patient ever in trouble with police needing help from social agency	17		
Marriage ended in legal separation or divorce	14.8 (% marriages)		
Currently unemployed	Females	25.6	
	Males	36.4	
Unemployed for six months or more	Females	9.7	
	Males	18.2	
Significant debts in past year	28.3		

It seems that overcrowding was certainly more common in DSH patients than expected, but the vast majority of them did not in fact live in such conditions. The relationship between immigrant status and DSH demonstrated by ecological study also appeared less impressive according to direct interviews: immigrants were not represented amongst DSH patients any more often than would have been expected from their proportion of the city population as a whole. This means that the positive correlation between the proportion of immigrants and the incidence of DSH in the various wards must indicate only an indirect relationship between the two. These two examples serve to illustrate the fact that ecological studies, useful as they are in emphasizing areas of greatest need, may produce misleading conclusions regarding the individuals at risk unless they are interpreted in the light of information obtained directly from a representative sample of the patients themselves.

The findings from Bristol are consistent with those from other British centres (Bancroft et al., 1975; Holding et al., 1977). DSH is more prevalent in the lower social classes: in Edinburgh there is an elevenfold difference between rates in classes I and II and class V. The rates in classes IV and V have increased progressively whereas those in I and II have remained stable with a marginal increase in class III since 1968. Overcrowding has recently become less obvious as a concomitant of DSH in Edinburgh and in 1974 the DSH admission rates in those who had not lived in overcrowded conditions were identical with those who had done so. Distribution of DSH throughout Edinburgh resembles that in Bristol in showing a high-rate central area of poor social conditions followed by peripheral interwar housing estates noted for their diversity of social problems. A low incidence is associated with middle class owner-occupied suburbs and there is over a sixfold difference between the highest and lowest rate wards.

The divorced usually show the highest rates of DSH in both sexes, in contrast to the widowed in whom rates are low. The significance of marital status is difficult to assess because of its age-related nature as well as difficulty in delineating the various groups involved. In Edinburgh men aged 35 years and older who are single have higher rates than the married, whereas the reverse applies to women. In Oxford exceptionally high rates have been found in teenage wives, in single, widowed, and divorced women aged 24 to 35 years, and in single men aged 35 to 45 years.

We have so far been considering only very crude indices of the social background of DSH, ones which may have little or indeed misleading significance with regards to the individual patient. Further direct information was obtained through interviews in our Bristol series

(Morgan *et al.*, 1975) with regards to early family life as well as chronic unemployment and financial difficulties. Evidence of early family disturbance in the form of long-lasting separation from one or more parents before the age of 15 years was found in 34 per cent. of the men and 26 per cent. of the women. This finding resembles that of Birtchnell (1970b) who found a significantly raised incidence of early parental loss through bereavement in persons who had attempted suicide when compared with controls. Other indices which included history of delinquency and aggressive behaviour revealed that antisocial behaviour had occurred at some time in the past more often than would have been expected: a criminal record was possessed by 30 per cent. of men though far less commonly by women (6 per cent.), and previous imprisonment had occurred in 14 and 5 per cent. respectively. These figures of course concern only a minority of DSH patients, though we can at least assume that in this particular subgroup social disruption has been a significant previous feature. Twenty-nine per cent. were judged to show evidence of personality disorder, which also of course implies chronic or recurrent disruption of their lives. Employment figures must also be interpreted carefully because they may reflect no more than general social difficulties in the community, but at the time of our study there was a fivefold increase in the proportion of unemployment in DSH patients compared with the national average, when the situation in Bristol was no different from that in the country as a whole. Of those who had worked in the previous year a third had changed their jobs and about two-thirds had experienced financial difficulties, 28 per cent. incurring significant debts.

Any assessment of background predisposing factors is grossly limited by deficiencies in available data. Furthermore, whilst our findings seem to have relevance to some DSH patients, they apply only to a minority, and it might be grossly misleading to generalize from them to the DSH problem as a whole, which undoubtedly is heterogeneous in aetiology: e.g. a history of antisocial behaviour which is relatively common in young male DSH patients must have somewhat dubious relevance with regards to young teenage females, who form a high proportion of the DSH problem as a whole.

9.2 Concomitants

Situational factors

We can of course reconstruct the events of the situation surrounding DSH by subsequently interviewing the patients and other key persons. If this approach is adopted it is necessary to avoid several pitfalls. We should take care not to generalize from the minority to the remainder; nor should we interpret the stress of a social situation according to our own preconceived ideas. Further, we cannot assume that the patients' reconstructions are necessarily objective and unedited.

Evaluation of living conditions of DSH patients illustrates some of these difficulties. The ecological approach suggested on the basis of a statistical association between the distribution of DSH and overcrowding in Bristol that there may be a relationship between the two. Direct interviews show, however, that only 7 per cent. of DSH patients actually live in overcrowded conditions, though they were of course found most commonly in areas where overcrowding was greatest. During direct interview very few (less than 2 per cent.) blamed accommodation difficulties such as overcrowding as a major cause of recent upset. In fact a somewhat greater proportion (10 per cent.) lived alone rather than in overcrowded conditions.

Direct interviews revealed that altogether 64 per cent. described some major recent upsetting event (Table 13). Twenty-nine per cent. could not

TABLE 13   Recent upsetting events in non-fatal deliberate self-harm

	Percentage ($N = 368$)
Disharmony with	
'key other' person	40
with other relatives	10
Anxiety regarding work	
and employment	5
Financial difficulties	5
Physical pain/illness	4
No recent upset	20
Depression	9
Social isolation	5
Miscellaneous (housing, difficulties, bereavement, repercussions of alcohol intake, gambling, or criminal behaviour)	2
	100

Source: Morgan *et al.*, 1975.

specify any particular difficulty, some of these (9 per cent.) saying that they had felt depressed and life in general was too much for them. By far the most common cause given (50 per cent.) was some kind of interpersonal upset with a key other person, sometimes of serious degree, such as a husband leaving home, though not infrequently apparently a trivial event, such as a boyfriend being late for a date. A sense of personal isolation (which can of course be experienced whatever the living density) was very common, 45 per cent. regarding themselves as not having a close friend and 35 per cent. feeling a sense of personal loneliness at all times. The general impression from these findings is that DSH is a heterogeneous problem, certainly with regards to its social characteristics. It may be that the predominant difficulties involved vary according to the living situation and social class, even though the final common pathway is DSH. This is supported by our findings that DSH patients who live in Bristol city centre differ in several ways from those living elsewhere (Table 14): they were younger, more socially mobile, having moved address in the previous six months, lived away from relatives more often, and were more likely to be either overcrowded or living in bedsitters.

The importance of situational factors has also been highlighted by the study of Paykel, Prusoff, and Myers (1975) in Newhaven, Connecticut, in which life events preceding DSH were categorized and compared with those in two control series, one of depressives and the other from the normal general population. DSH patients showed four times as many events compared with the general population, with a peaking in the previous month. Most types of life event appeared relevant compared with the general population but the excess over depressives selectively

TABLE 14   DSH patients from central 'high-rate' areas of Bristol

	DSH patients from central area, % ($N = 67$)	DSH patients from remainder of city, % ($N = 301$)	Significance level of difference
Below 35 years of age	82	62	< 0.01
In bedsitter	21	4	< 0.001
At present address less than six months	48	21	< 0.001
Living away from relative	48	27	< 0.01
Overcrowded conditions	13	5	< 0.05

Source: Morgan *et al.*, 1975.

involved events with threatening implications, including undesirable events, those regarded as stressful, and those outside the respondent's control. A strong and immediate relationship between DSH and life events does seem to have been established.

Personal factors

The *mental state* of patients at the time of DSH can usually be evaluated only retrospectively after recovery from the effects of the drug overdose or physical injury. When this is done a general picture is obtained which is consistent with that deduced from the study of social concomitants: commonly this is one of persons rendered vulnerable in various ways and who react adversely to interpersonal and social stresses.

The psychiatric assessments of our Bristol series using interviews soon after the event are shown in Table 15; they are typical of findings from other centres. Commonly a small proportion, up to 12 per cent. are found to suffer from major functional psychotic mental illness and this was most often depressive. When organic brain disorders were found they were usually related to alcohol abuse, more commonly in men (16 per cent.) than women (5 per cent.). The most common disorder was reactive depression (39 per cent. of men and 59 per cent. of women), indicating that as a result of some upsetting event, serious significant depressive symptoms developed. Making such a diagnosis can be a somewhat arbitrary matter. We were so impressed by the frequency and severity of depressive symptoms that it seemed inappropriate to minimize them, a view supported by the findings from our use of the Middlesex Hospital Questionnaire which showed high scores on depression and anxiety scales, males exceeding those in females. Personality disorder, found in 42 per cent. of men and 22 per cent. of women, had often led to recurrent social disruption over some years, with obvious relevance to long-term predisposition and the final act of DSH.

The relationship between the use of alcohol and DSH is worthy of more detailed discussion (Table 16). It seems that far more women (75 per cent.) than men (48 per cent.) had been able to restrict their alcohol intake to uncomplicated social drinking. About a quarter of men and 7 per cent. of women showed evidence of alcohol intake sufficient to interfere with the smooth running of their lives. Recent increases in social drinking had occurred in 17 per cent. of men and 7 per cent. of women, and this provided a useful indirect source of evidence for concomitant stresses. Apart from its chronic disruptive effects, alcohol may play a significant part in precipitating DSH. It had been taken within six hours preceding

TABLE 15 Psychiatric diagnosis patients admitted to hospital (some patients had more than one diagnosis)

Diagnosis	Total series N = 337 (%)	Male N = 114 (%)	Female N = 223 (%)
Mental illness absent	33 (10)	6 (5)	27 (12)
Personality disorder	97 (29)	48 (42)	49 (22)
Neurosis	212 (63)	64 (56)	148 (66)
Neurotic (reactive) depression	175 (52)	44 (39)	131 (59)
Other	37 (11)	20 (17)	17 (8)
Functional psychosis	42 (12)	16 (14)	26 (11)
Manic depressive psychosis	17 (5)	6 (5)	11 (5)
Reactive depressive psychosis	14 (4)	4 (3)	10 (4)
Other affective psychoses	3 (1)	1 (1)	2 (1)
Schizophrenia	7 (2)	4 (3)	3 (1)
Paranoid psychosis	1 (<1)	1 (1)	—
Organic psychosis	32 (10)	19 (17)	13 (6)
Dementia	2 (1)	1 (1)	1 (<1)
Alcoholic psychosis	28 (8)	18 (16)	10 (5)
Associated with endocrine disorder	2 (1)	—	2 (1)
Alcohol abuse	61 (18)	41 (36)	20 (9)
Alcohol addiction	35 (10)	23 (20)	12 (5)
Heavy drinking (habitual or episodic)	26 (8)	18 (16)	8 (4)

Source: Morgan *et al.*, 1975.

110

the event by 55 per cent. of men, significantly more frequently than by women (25 per cent.) and often in amounts greater than usual. We know that alcohol by direct effect is likely to reduce inhibitions and increase the likelihood of aggressive behaviour, whilst the depression of alcohol withdrawal may be accentuated in someone who has real life problems; its relevance as a predisposing and precipitating factor in self-harm is therefore obvious. It was found to be much more common in DSH which occurred in the high-rate central area than elsewhere in Bristol.

Motivation is just as difficult to assess as any other aspect of DSH which we have so far discussed. Retrospective evaluation is fraught with many problems of reliability. Nevertheless, a certain consistency is found whenever the reasons that patients give for harming themselves are looked at systematically.

The most striking impression is that while some patients seem to have had serious conscious intention of killing themselves this does not apply to the majority, at least with regards to motivation which they are prepared to acknowledge. Our own findings (Table 17) reveal that whilst a sizeable proportion subsequently said that at the time they had wanted to die (46 per cent. of men and 34 per cent. of women), by next day or soon afterwards a much smaller proportion regretted not doing so (17 per cent. of men and 10 per cent. of women). Only a little over one-quarter in either sex expected that they would die. In less than 10 per cent. was it evident that there had been serious intention to die, e.g. as demonstrated by making a will or actively trying to avoid discovery. Fourteen per cent.

TABLE 16   DSH: pattern of alcohol intake in the previous three months

Alcohol intake	Male N = 121 (%)	Female N = 247 (%)	Significance level of male/ female difference
Always abstinent	11 (9)	25 (10)	NS
Uncomplicated social drinking	58 (48)	185 (75)	< 0.001
Increased social drinking	20 (17)	17 (7)	< 0.01
Problem drinking	29 (24)	17 (7)	< 0.001
Uncertain	3 (3)	3 (1)	—
Alcohol intake within six hours preceding self-harm:			
Usual amount	34 (28)	37 (15)	< 0.001
More than usual amount	32 (25)	25 (10)	< 0.001

Source: Morgan *et al.*, 1975.

warned others before the event, 44 per cent. afterwards. Again we obtained the impression that although a small proportion are probably failed suicides, the majority do not entertain serious ideas of self-destruction or if they do they quickly change their minds after the event. Although half the patients had toyed with the idea of self-harm in the previous month, the majority (65 per cent.) acted more or less impulsively when it eventually occurred, subsequently denying that they had made plans during the same day. A general picture begins to emerge: although DSH motivation is complex and heterogeneous, most commonly it is an impulsive act in the context of some upsetting event which precipitates acute emotional upset, most frequently depression in someone who though vulnerable is otherwise not seriously mentally ill. Frequently it is facilitated by the effects of recent alcohol intake and/or chronic abuse of alcohol.

Two other studies have considered motivation in DSH in considerable detail (Bancroft, Skrimshire, and Simkin, 1976; Birtchnell and deAlarcon, 1971a). They too found that only a minority of episodes seemed to be associated with conscious and deliberate suicidal motivation as measured by an acknowledged wish to die at the time. This being so, they proceeded to investigate what the real motivation might be. In order to overcome the resistances which patients undoubtedly have in trying to remember motives after the event, whether this be due to fear of rejection by others, repression of angry feelings, or a failure to admit to the self the full implications of what had happened, various possible motives were

TABLE 17   Attitudes to self-harm at the time of act
(percentage of interviewed patients)

Attitude	Male	Female
Wanted to die	46.3	34.4
Expected to die	28.9	25.5
Preparations made for death, e.g. making a will	5.8	3.6
Active precautions taken against discovery	7.4	1.6
Regrets not killing self (at time of interview)	17.4	10.5
Left suicide note	21.5	16.2
Planned act more than six hours before	11.6	10.9

Source: Morgan et al., 1975.

suggested to individuals soon after episodes of DSH. Birtchnell and deAlarcon noted an important sex difference: fewer women expressed a wish to die and consequently more of them appeared to act impulsively; over half the women had contemplated the suicidal act either not at all or only for a matter of minutes beforehand compared with 18.5 per cent. of men. They concluded that men are more reluctant to 'attempt suicide', they think about it longer, need to be more depressed, and when they do so they are more determined and more often succeed. In view of the many difficulties in reconstructing motivation, particularly with regards to the estimation of suicidal feelings, Birtchnell and deAlarcon urge caution lest we underestimate incidence of these in DSH. Their study was replicated by Bancroft, Skrimshire, and Simkin (1976) who explored reasons, feelings, and expected effects. Some of their findings are illustrated in Table 18, and it is clear that they have a general similarity to those already discussed. Some consistency was found in the way reasons grouped together. The depressive or 'self-referring' were worried about the future, sorry or ashamed about something, saw themselves as failures in life, and

TABLE 18   Motivation in deliberate self-harm (DSH)

Choice of reason other than 'wish to die' (%)	
Seek help	33
Escape situation	42
Relief from state of mind	52
Influence someone	19
None of these	18
Feelings at the time (%)	
Worried	46
Angry	32
Lonely	58
Sorry	27
Failed	52
None	9
Expected effect of the attempt (%)	
Show someone how much you love them	20
Make things easier for others	27
Make people sorry	15
Frighten or get your own back	6
None	42

Source: Bancroft, Skrimshire, and Simkin, 1976.

sought relief from a state of mind. This appeared to be distinguished from the 'other referring' group who wanted to influence someone, make others sorry, frighten or get their own back on someone, or show how much they love another person. Another group showed both these characteristics and yet others clearly had wanted to die and just make things easier for others. A 'wish to die' did not correlate highly with depressive-type symptoms and was negatively associated with anger and escape but more strongly with 'make easy for others' or 'show how much you love someone'. Thus, apart from indicating true suicidal motives in a few, it was suggested that the 'wish to die' may be used as part of an appeal for help. Other persons respond most readily and sympathetically to this expressed reason for DSH (Ramon, Bancroft, and Skrimshire, 1975), and it has been found to correlate positively with the presence of situational problems. These studies represent important first steps in our understanding of motivation in DSH, opening up a research area which may lead the way to more effective treatment and prediction of outcome.

10

CAUSES

In our discussion of individual and environmental correlates of DSH we have been careful to avoid unjustifiable assumptions that such factors are necessarily causal. The data discussed so far are grossly limited in quality by methodological research problems. It is clearly very unsatisfactory to examine causes entirely in terms of averaged data obtained from large series of DSH patients: such an approach encourages the concept of stereotypes which pays little regard to the heterogeneous nature of DSH and may be of little help in the understanding of the individual patient. We must therefore look more closely at the psychopathology involved and attempt to interpret it in the light of the correlates described in the previous chapter. In our search for causes we must of course try to explain some very remarkable features of the DSH problem, such as its dramatic epidemic-like increase in incidence since the early 1960s, the fact that it affects females more than males, and its marked variation in distribution throughout the social classes and between various parts of an urban area.

Our discussion will be concerned first with motivational factors which apply at the time DSH occurs. After this we will examine those which are antecedent and predisposing and these will of course concern individual and psychological difficulties, interpersonal and social problems, and finally wider influences in society as a whole.

10.1 Motivating Factors

Intrapsychic

It is clear that a small proportion of DSH patients are in fact failed suicides: These amount to about 10 per cent. of all persons who declare themselves at hospitals following an episode of deliberate self-harm. The

114

failed suicides have usually made determined attempts on their lives, intended not to survive, and they continue to have strong suicidal wishes after physical recovery. It is in this group that severe depressive symptoms and other forms of mental illness are most common; their detection through efficient evaluation of the DSH patient is of the greatest importance in suicide prevention.

In the remainder, the motivation involved appears to be much more complex, and conscious preoccupation with suicide either beforehand or at the time of DSH is by no means typical. Less than half of all DSH patients subsequently admit to having wanted to die, only a little more than a quarter expected to die, and usually by the next day almost 90 per cent. are glad that they have survived. We have of course noted the marked ambivalence which is discernible in the behaviour of suicides during the weeks before they kill themselves, and in evaluating DSH patients we should be careful not to discount the importance of true suicidal ideation mainly because it is denied after the event. Marked clinical improvement can occur following a serious episode of DSH, even in very depressed individuals, and quite serious physical complications may be borne with equanimity. Stengel (1952) suggested that the explanation for this lies in the 'ordeal character' of DSH. This is seen as a gamble, a test between the life-preserving tendencies, on the one hand, and the destructive impulses, on the other; the outcome of survival, even as an invalid, is then accepted without demur. It is indeed remarkable how enduring such acceptance of disabilities may be. One of our DSH patients sustained severe burns and contractures of his fingers when he burnt himself by holding an electric fire and another young student badly fractured his left arm in jumping from a ward window; both have since shown considerably more psychological resilience in spite of their newly developed serious physical disabilities.

About half of all DSH patients explain the event in terms of seeking relief blindly from an intolerable state of mind or a stressful situation, having no conscious concern for the consequences though feeling sure that self-destruction would be unlikely. It is probably not fortuitous that the great majority choose for self-poisoning agents which have been presented to them as safe and effective solutions for troubled states of mind. Recent alcohol intake commonly facilitates DSH by increasing the likelihood that interpersonal conflict, depressive mood swings, and impulsive 'acting-out' behaviour will occur. An alcohol-induced amnesia or dissociative states may also be relevant (Mayfield and Montgomery, 1972; Ryback, 1971).

In looking for causes of DSH it is important to consider self-laceration separately in order to discern psychopathological mechanisms which may be peculiar to it and which are not shared by those who take drug over-dosage. Even within the group of self-lacerators causes may be multiple, and differing impressions tend to be gained through the study of highly selected groups. Self-laceration can be a particularly difficult manage-ment problem in hospital wards and institutions, especially when it is repetitive and becomes the subject of imitative behaviour, whereas it might appear trivial when seen in hospital Accident and Emergency Departments. Ballinger (1971) has estimated that 15 per cent. of patients in a hospital for the mentally handicapped injured themselves during a period of one month, usually by some form of skin laceration, frequently related to frustration, annoyance, or boredom. The more common stereotype of the self-lacerator and the processes involved has been described by Podvall (1969):

> In the face of some unknown precipitant, of which they claim (and seem to prefer) total ignorance, they experience a sudden and intense physical discomfort and an impending feeling that something 'has to happen'. From the physical agitation coupled with progressive isolation, an act of almost cool determination is planned and executed: a bodily part (usually predetermined) is mortified. Out of paralysed relatedness comes significant action. Then a sense of calm is restored; the patient is able to relax, sleep, and is completely indifferent to the injured part.

Other American writers have typified the self-lacerator who presents to private psychiatric hospitals as an attractive young woman aged 23, unmarried, usually above average in intelligence, and having attended college. She tends to be a heavy alcohol and tranquillizer user, often gets drunk on excursions from hospital, and invariably has difficulties in interpersonal relationships. Our Bristol survey demonstrated that at least in one provincial English city, men outnumber women amongst patients presenting at hospital Accident and Emergency Departments following self-laceration, suggesting that the 'beautiful and female' stereotype may be only one amongst many.

Intensive individual case work suggests that self-laceration may involve an altered state of consciousness akin to a dissociative state, sometimes accompanied by depersonalization at the time that laceration is carried out. As a result the patient may be unaware of the act of cutting and is perhaps also oblivious of surroundings, though the self-injury is usually strictly limited in extent and carefully carried out. There may be no experience of pain until after the event when there is subjective relief of tension mixed with feelings of disgust and regret at what has happened.

This remarkable though transient mental disturbance has prompted some American writers to suggest that it is in the nature of a schizophrenic psychotic reaction (Graff and Mallin, 1967; Ping Nie Pao, 1969). The process is then seen as one of differential regression with suspension of consciousness, though motor control is well preserved, leading to an act which is motivated by sadistic and masochistic feelings. The high incidence of tranquillizer and alcohol abuse said to be found in these individuals may reflect their need to obtain relief from tension and a search for major changes in consciousness of the kind prescribed. Alcohol intake immediately before self-laceration may of course itself influence awareness and subsequent recall. An English study (Gardner and Gardner, 1975) has, however, emphasized that major changes in consciousness such as those described may occur in only about a third of episodes of self-laceration. In many the process may have an obsessional compulsive quality, with typical initial resistance and a sense of relief immediately afterwards. A high incidence of obsessionality, as measured clinically and by formal psychological tests, as well as for phobic symptoms and narcissistic bodily preoccupation, has been reported by some authors (Gardner and Gardner, 1975; McKerracher, Loughnane, and Watson, 1968). This syndrome has been termed 'compulsive autotomy' (James, 1975) and often occurs in a setting of severe personality problems characterized by impulsive aggressive behaviour. Such individuals may present with widespread though superficial self-inflicted skin lacerations or burns (Figure 11). Early emotional deprivation is probably an important causal factor in this group.

The occurrence of outbreaks of self-laceration in prisons or in institutions where freedom of movement is strictly limited highlights the relevance of imitation in leading to such behaviour under certain circumstances. The immediate impact that it has on others also indicates that in some instances there might also be an element of secondary gain aimed at coercion or situational avoidance. Although the frequent occurrence of anaesthesia during the process of self-laceration has often been stressed, in some individuals who have major identity problems the injury may signify a deliberate self-infliction of pain as a way of confirming that they have any feelings at all.

Appeal and communicational effect

DSH cannot be understood entirely in terms of intrapsychic pathology. There is a massive body of evidence testifying to its close relationship with interpersonal and social events, and not merely as a blind reaction to them. The response from other key persons is usually immediate, and if

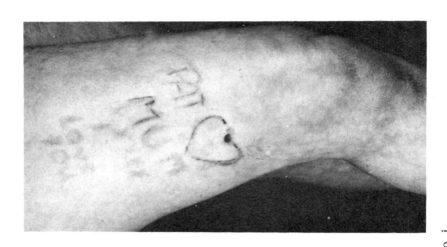

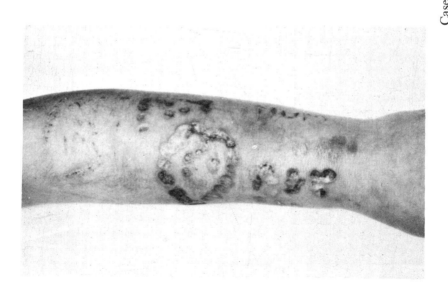

Case no. i

FIGURE 11. Self inflicted injuries. (Reproduced by kind permission of Dr. I. Pierce James)

119

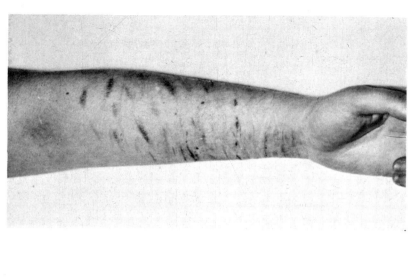

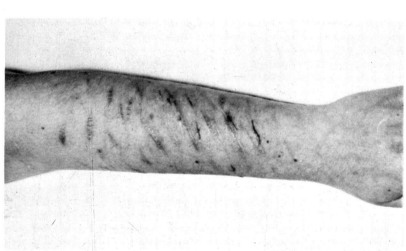

Case no. 2

Figure 11 continued

120

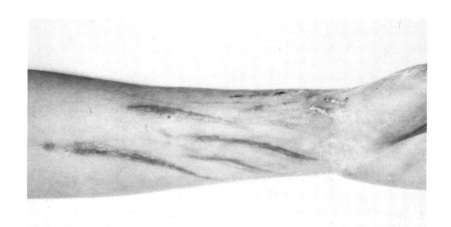

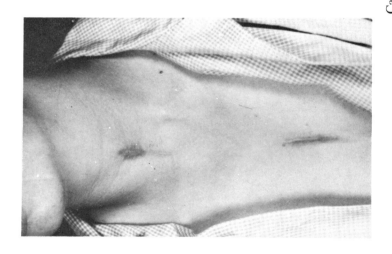

Case no 3

Figure 11 continued

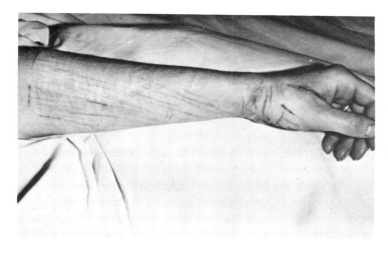

Case no. 5

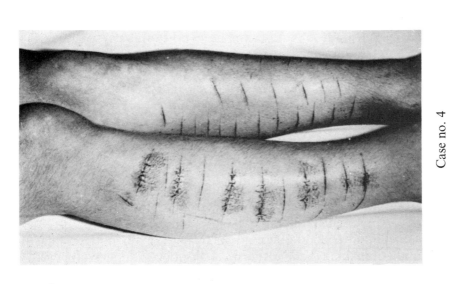

Case no. 4

Figure 11 continued

only in terms of hospital admission the life situation is changed dramatically. To what extent can we explain DSH as a form of communication, one which is aimed consciously or unconsciously at achieving changes which are not possible by more conventional means? Stengel (1952) was perhaps the first to emphasize the 'appeal' effect of DSH. He summarized the situation in the following way:

> To the patient the suicide attempt stands for death and survival and often for a new beginning. To the relatives it stands for bereavement and mourning. It sometimes creates the peculiar situation in which somebody who has died and revived is with us alive while we are mourning him. All this engenders a tendency to renewal and revision of human relationships on the part of all concerned.

Stengel also comments on the frequency with which the 'suicide attempt' was found to have been the only effective alarm signal to mobilize long overdue medical and social help. This applied both to physical and mental illness; he noted a tendency to deny the morbid nature of mental change on the part of the patient's close associates as well as an almost limitless tolerance of psychiatric symptoms.

More recently the situation has been summarized succinctly by a Lancet (1974) leading article: 'Some pervasive influence is affecting increasing numbers of people. That influence may be the knowledge that the wish to die, made obvious, can be a powerful way of releasing intolerable stresses or generating concern.'

There has been little systematic study of the way in which others respond to DSH. Stengel suggested that it may be a useful trigger stimulus which achieves change in the status quo and mobilizes constructive forces, though it is equally true that DSH, especially when it is resorted to recurrently, may lead to deterioration in the life situation either by estranging other key individuals who feel coerced and blackmailed or through resulting economic difficulties which may even include the loss of a job. DSH is undoubtedly a maladaptive form of behaviour if only because its repercussions with regard to personal safety and the response of others is so unpredictable.

Occasional blind anger at others is seen to be the main motivation with the intention of making them feel sorry, as Whitlock and Schapira (1967) point out in illustrating the common unstable adolescent crisis situation:

> ... usually young girls who have little emotional control but do not otherwise show any recognisable psychiatric disorder. After some comparatively trivial disappointment, frustration or difference of opinion with an

older person, usually a parent, they make a suicide attempt during a mood of deep but brief depression more than tinged with rage or resentment. Many patients in this category admitted that the induction of guilt in those whom they blamed for their distress, was a prominent motive for the suicide attempt.

We have also noted previously that the expressed motive also frequently implies concern and an anxiety for others or a wish to communicate a need for help.

Kreitman and his colleagues (Kreitman, Smith and Eng-Seong Tan, 1969, 1970) have pointed out that the communication or language aspect of DSH is of great importance. Differential response in the community may go some way towards explaining the gross variation in incidence of DSH amongst the various subcultural groups and social classes. Arguing that the 'signal function' of DSH cannot be resolved merely by reference to conscious intent, they examined the behaviour of relatives and friends of DSH patients. They found that a significantly greater number of these contacts has been admitted previously to hospital because of DSH than would have been expected in comparable groups from the general population. The effect was most marked in young female self-poisoning patients and it may be significant that such persons account for most of the rise in DSH incidence of recent years. Has this been due to a 'contagion' factor with case-to-case spread through the communication effect of self-harm? Only further research will clarify the full implications of this question: we still do not know the precise function of the DSH signal nor the circumstances which promote such imitative behaviour. It is relevant that 18 per cent. of our Bristol series were aware of one or more episodes of DSH in a first-degree relative. A concurrent study of DSH in Bristol school children by Walker (1978) showed 20 per cent. in this category.

In our discussion of attitudes to DSH we have noted that others, whether they be hospital staff, relatives, or friends, often express hostility and lack of sympathy. Frequently a distinction is made between 'genuine' and 'non-genuine' acts of DSH; those which appear to represent a serious suicide bid and are associated with a wish to die tend to be accepted more readily than others which may appear trivial. Stengel warned us of the fallacy of such an approach and he declared firmly that there is no fundamental difference between 'genuine' and 'non-genuine' suicide attempts. The appeal function whereby the act seems to be aimed at others is common to all episodes of DSH in some degree, though the patient is often unware of it and it should not be regarded as an index of low risk. Undoubtedly some episodes of DSH represent primarily a superficial attempt at manipulating the life situation by coercing others or perhaps avoiding responsibilities and the repercussions of ill-judged behaviour. Stengel was certainly correct in warning us that we should be on our guard not to allow such considerations to monopolize our attitude to the DSH patient, because by generalizing in this way we run the risk of rejecting many who are in real need of help.

10.2 Predisposition

The search for more distant predisposing causes of DSH is more difficult still: not only is the relationship between cause and effect much more attenuated but our unsophisticated methods of detection and measurement of psychological factors impose limits of their own, the usual approach involving a retrospective examination of case histories of DSH patients leading to averaged data denoting the proportion which possess various clinical and social characteristics. In a heterogeneous problem such as DSH this approach presents many difficulties, encouraging generalization from a few to the remainder thereby leading to stereotypes which ignore a significant number of patients who may have very different characteristics yet are not taken into account because they are relatively few in number.

Our earlier discussion of ecological studies considered these methodological problems in some detail, demonstrating how important it is to interpret findings in the light of data obtained directly from patient interviews. Causal theories must account for the remarkable variation in incidence amongst the social classes and its very high incidence in some parts of an urban area compared with others. In Bristol it is concentrated in the city centre and those more peripheral areas where council estates have developed. These are parts where social problems and living stresses abound, as measured by the proportion of housing difficulties, children in care, and the incidence of violent crimes. In spite of this ecological correlation between DSH and living conditions we cannot infer a causal connection between the two. It may be that the association is an indirect one, such as the migration of vulnerable personalities into the high-rate areas. We have noted the greater degree of social isolation and mobility and loss of contact with family in DSH patients living in the high-rate central areas of Bristol compared with those living elsewhere. Alternatively the key factor may be differential exposure to the agent used in self-poisoning: to take one example, we know little about the differential rates of prescribing habits of doctors throughout the various social classes and urban districts.

Similar caution must apply to our interpretation of the increased incidence of aggressive antisocial behaviour in DSH patients. In those who possess these characteristics we may infer a certain degree of disruption in the pattern of their lives, but the majority do not possess such a history. It may be that aggressive individuals constitute a discrete subgroup of DSH patients in which psychopathological factors are quite different from those of the remainder. Alternatively these findings may provide a clue to the cause of DSH in general, whereby the degree of self-control particularly with regard to aggressive acting-out is in some degree impaired.

The significance of early parental loss is worthy of more detailed consideration because of its theoretical and practical implications. In our Bristol studies a separation of six months or longer due to whatever cause was taken as the index of permanent separation before the age of 15. Several other investigations based on parental death have produced similar findings and they have been discussed by Birtchnell (1970a, 1970b). It seems clear that significantly more DSH patients suffer prolonged parental absence during their childhood than would be expected in the general population. What relationship does this have to the subsequent DSH behaviour? Does it predispose to depression or does the early experience of loss or bereavement make it more likely that under stress such individual then selectively choose a form of threatened loss whose impact they themselves had felt keenly at an earlier age? It is of interest here that in our Bristol study we found early separation from the mother figure to be a predictor of DSH repetition during the following year.

Kreitman (1977) has argued forcibly that if we are to improve our understanding of the DSH problem it is important that we look for subgroups which are themselves homogeneous in causation or which at least share major causal factors. Using age as an easily measured index he has looked at differences between DSH patients of three major age groups: the young (15 to 34 years), middle aged (35 to 54 years), and older individuals (over 55 years). Useful age-related characteristics were demonstrated, of value not only in DSH assessment but also in discerning causal patterns. Suicidal risk increased with age, more markedly and beginning earlier in men. Alcohol misuse was a dominant problem in middle age, again particularly in men. This approach also drew attention to the older patients, a relatively neglected group, demonstrating that even here there was quite a high incidence (25 per cent.) of longstanding personality difficulties. It is also of interest that although suicide risk was age related the rate of DSH repetition was not.

10.3 Factors in Society at Large

At no point in our discussion so far have we really gained any insight into possible reasons for the epidemic-like increase of DSH in most Western countries since the early 1960s. The imitative contagion-like effect in younger persons undoubtedly is relevant here, but why has this form of behaviour been chosen instead of others? What new influences are there in society especially concerning young adults and particularly relevant to females?

At the present time we can only resort to conjecture with regard to these important issues. It may be that the traditional family group has become less effective as young persons have become more likely to move away and lead socially mobile lives in high-density urban areas. When crises occur they have fewer relatives and friends to whom they can turn. The problems facing youth have certainly changed markedly during the last few decades, early emancipation occurring in a setting where previously accepted formal rules of interpersonal and moral conduct are severely questioned. Young women often find themselves in a dilemma when their emancipation is hindered by continued restraints such as unequal job opportunities or domestic commitments which are not shared by their male partners. It may be that there has been an increased tendency to 'act-out' dissatisfactions and to signal distress in a clear unequivocal way such as by taking an overdose when all else has failed. Perhaps self-assertion has become more common than quiet though dissatisfied acceptance.

It may also be relevant that society's attitude to suicide and so to deliberate self-harm have become more tolerant in recent years. In doing so have we encouraged individuals in crisis to use self-harm as a signal of distress? It may be that the increased incidence of DSH is the price we pay for lessened social control and authoritarianism.

One further very important consideration remains. The explosive increase in incidence of DSH of recent years is frequently likened to an epidemic. What about the 'infective' agent? Most of the increased incidence has been due to overdoses with one or more psychotropic drugs, usually obtained through medical prescription. Have these agents become more available in recent years? They most certainly have. Figure 12 illustrates the way in which the numbers of medical prescriptions for tranquillizers, non-barbiturate hypnotics, and antidepressants have gradually increased in England and Wales since 1960, though there has been a fall in prescriptions for barbiturates. Figure 12 also shows how the pattern of drug misuse in DSH has changed during this time. It does seem that availability through medical prescription is mirrored closely by the frequency with which a drug is used for the purpose of deliberate overdosage. The proportion of barbiturates used in this way has fallen at a time when there has been a reciprocal increase in misuse of other psychotropic drugs.

This is compelling evidence for an association between the incidence of DSH and the availability of psychotropic drugs through medical prescription. What is the precise significance of this association? Are such drugs used inappropriately as a panacea for individuals whose problems are not resolved by them? If so the scene is then set for deliberate

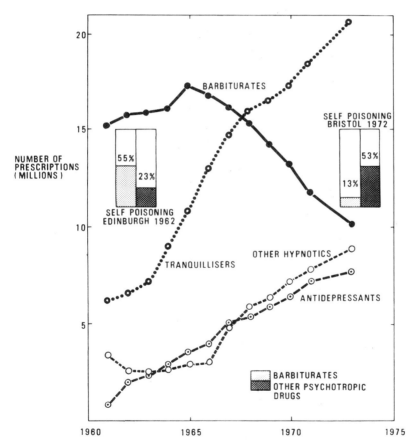

FIGURE 12. Trends in national prescriptions of psychotropic drugs and methods of non-fatal self poisoning 1961–73. (Sources: Annual Reports D.H.S.S. Kessel, 1965; Morgan *et al.*, 1975)

128

overdosage when further crises occur, because the agent is immediately available. DSH may indeed be a reflection of anger and hostility, not only against other key persons but also against the doctor whose remedy has so clearly failed. The medical prescription of psychotropic drugs needs careful review and it is a sad reflection on the pharmaceutical industry, having spent so much on promoting these drugs, that we know nothing about the incidence of DSH complicating their prescription or the social and clinical conditions under which overdose is most likely to occur. We will return to this in our later discussion of DSH prevention.

11

NATURAL HISTORY

When we come to assess how serious DSH really is we encounter considerable diversity of opinion on the matter. Some regard it as being on the whole benign and trivial. They point out that the great majority of DSH patients survive apparently unharmed; and DSH may be seen as a useful safety valve for emotional difficulties which build up in the face of the stresses of present-day life, perhaps even constructive in its ultimate effect. Closely allied to this attitude is the implication that if it did not occur, something much more dangerous would take its place. Others take the opposite view, pointing out that apart from the heavy and increasing load which it places upon hospital services, DSH leaves considerable damage in its wake, both physical and psychological.

Study of the natural history or course of DSH is essential in our approach to these attitudes. The follow-up and assessment of outcome of DSH in a representative sample of patients allows us to evaluate its effects on their psychological and physical well-being as well as their relationships and their life situation in general. Knowledge of its natural history may also help in the understanding of DSH in other ways. Classification of patients according to outcome may produce groupings which provide us with an insight into the various underlying causes. By extending a study prospectively over a period of time, the relationship between further DSH and environmental difficulties is of course clarified. Detailed knowledge of the full spectrum of DSH outcome also permits its correlation with various personal and situational factors which precede DSH: in this way predictive scales may be constructed thereby assisting clinical management by detecting individuals who are at particular risk in various ways.

A follow-up study needs to pay particular attention to certain methodological difficulties. It must of course obtain information with regards to a sufficient number of patients to make the conclusions from them reliable and valid with regards to the problem as a whole. This usually means that well over 90 per cent. of patients should be traced and accounted for. Further, information should be obtained where possible through direct interviews, and the follow-up period should be sufficiently long to reveal long-term trends in outcome. Our Bristol follow-up study paid particular attention to these issues: 279 DSH patients were followed up after one to two years and only in nine cases (3 per cent.) was information completely unobtainable. Most patients (80 per cent.) were interviewed directly (Morgan *et al.*, 1976). We will refer to the findings from this study and compare them with others in the course of our discussion.

11.1 The Problem of Repetition

An act of DSH which brings an individual patient to hospital is by no means necessarily the only such event in his life. About half of DSH patients have a history of one or more previous episodes (Bancroft and Marsack, 1977; Morgan *et al.*, 1976) and a proportion will repeat it subsequently. Although it is in many ways a very restricted and incomplete measure of outcome after DSH, repetition does provide some crude index of response to treatment aimed at preventing further episodes. The greater the amount of repetition the more the risk of accidental fatal outcome from overdose or self-poisoning. Bancroft and Marsack (1977) have also suggested that successive episodes may become increasingly severe through a process of desensitization which permits progressively greater risks to be taken.

The repetition rate during the year after an episode of DSH in Bristol patients was found to be 25 per cent. in men and 23 per cent. in women. In men there was a marked clustering of repeats in the first month with only sporadic episodes subsequently; in women repeats also tended to be concentrated in the first few months, but less so than in men.

Follow-up studies of DSH from Oxford and Edinburgh suggest annual repetition rates between 15 and 34 per cent. in men and 10 and 20 per cent. in women. Bancroft and Marsack have emphasized that the great majority of repeats occur within the first year and more in the previous three months than in the remaining twenty-one during a two-year follow-up period. They distinguished three patterns of repetition:

(1) The chronic (a third) in whom overdosing is a habitual method of dealing with life difficulties. These have the highest number of previous episodes and are responsible for two-thirds of subsequent repetition.

(2) Clustering where two or more episodes occur within a few months

during prolonged stress, followed by avoidance of DSH for quite long periods.

(3) The 'one-off' in which a single episode of DSH occurs at a time of severe crisis, and repetition is rare.

It may well be that the underlying causes leading to DSH in these groups are very different and in particular the habitual chronic DSH patient has probably acquired distinct psychopathological attitudes through recurrent reinforcement.

Predicting repetition

When the preceding individual and social characteristics of DSH patients are matched with the number of subsequent repeat episodes it is possible to pick out those factors which are associated with increased risk of repetition. Table 19 illustrates the relevant findings in Bristol with regard to repetition of DSH at least once during a period of twelve months

TABLE 19   Risk factors for repetition of deliberate self-harm

	N	Males Repetition (%)	N	Females Repetition (%)
Previous psychiatric treatment	35	51	48	50
Previous episodes	48	50	69	48
Sociopathy	5	80	2	50
Alcohol problem	21	43	8	63
Personality disorder	30	50	29	31
Not living with relatives	23	43	32	28
Less than one year at present address	36	64	53	22
In debt	28	39	35	34
Unemployed	31	48	37	30
Social classes IV or V	32	47	46	30
Separated or divorced	20	45	31	29
Separated from mother before 15 years	21	48	22	41
Separated from father before 15 years	17	65	35	37
Not precipitated by upset	29	38	29	41
Regret surviving	15	53	15	40
All patients	75	32	140	23

Source: Morgan *et al.*, 1976.

132

(Morgan *et al.*, 1976). The incidence of each of these characteristics was determined in repeaters and non-repeaters and the differences expressed statistically at various levels of probability. In this way factors which distinguished repeaters and non-repeaters were picked out (Table 20).

Three factors which distinguished repeaters from the others (at less than 0.001 level of probability) were previous psychiatric treatment, a previous act of DSH, and a criminal record. Others associated at a lower level of statistical significance included social classes IV or V, early separation from mother, regrets at surviving, and serious alcohol or drug problems. Personality disorders also picked out repeaters, presumably implying chronic anteceding problems which were likely to continue subsequently: this probably also explains the finding that absence of obvious precipitating factor was also associated with repetition.

It was then shown that using a scale based on the three items which distinguished repeaters from non-repeaters at the 0.001 level, 77 per cent. of repeaters and 32 per cent. of non-repeaters scored two and three. The scale was applied to a second series of 179 patients and the findings were very similar: 72 per cent. repeaters scored two or three compared with 41 per cent. non-repeaters. In both series risk increased progressively with increasing score on the predictive scale.

TABLE 20 Factors significant for DSH repetition within twelve months of initial episode

	Repeaters $N = 56$	Non-repeaters $N = 159$
Factors significant at p < 0.001		
(a) Previous psychiatric treatment	49	62
(b) Previous act of DSH	42	65
(c) Criminal record	33	38
Factors significant at p < 0.01		
(d) Social classes IV and V	29	49
(e) Separation from spouse/cohabitee	16	19
(f) Separation from mother before age of 15	18	22
(g) Initial episode not precipitated by any upset	23	35
(h) Regret surviving	14	16
(i) Personality disorder	24	35
(j) Serious drink problem	14	15
(k) Drug dependence	8	3

Source: Morgan *et al.*, 1976.

There are important difficulties in the use of such a predictive scale in clinical practice. If only those patients who score one or more are taken on for treatment then practically all repeaters will be included. However, the scale allows only incomplete discrimination of repeaters and non-repeaters because 60 per cent. of non-repeaters also possess one or more of these risk factors. Repetition alone is in any case too narrow and inadequate an indication of outcome and it cannot be the sole criterion whereby a decision is made to treat. We will return to the problem of how to apply predictive scales when we discuss assessment and treatment.

Predictors of repetition determined through our Bristol studies resembled findings from Edinburgh (Buglass and Horton, 1974) and have been shown to be valid for several cohorts of patients. In both cities factors which were not associated with repetition included a diagnosis of depression, alcohol intake at the time of the act, early separation from the father, less than one year at previous address, overcrowding, in debt, a family member receiving psychiatric treatment, and disposal to inpatient psychiatric care. Most studies agree that the medical seriousness of DSH is also not related to subsequent non-fatal repetition although it may well be an index of suicide risk in the small proportion who subsequently kill themselves.

The general characteristics of repeaters has been summed up by Buglass and Horton (1974): they tend to be described as personality disorders, people who try to resolve their problems by excessive use of alcohol or drugs, have already experienced psychiatric attention, and in whose lives DSH is a recurrent theme. In comparison with non-repeaters they are predominantly of low social class and frequently unemployed, their previous history often includes a criminal conviction, and their personal relationships are marked by violence.

'First evers'

One of the problems of confining our attention to repetition is that it encourages us to fix our efforts on those who repeat DSH, perhaps to the exclusion of others. Undoubtedly patients who are more likely to repeat DSH need help, but their repetitive pattern of DSH is particularly difficult to influence and change for the better. They are more likely than others to be already committed to a chronic pattern of repetition: in fact the probability of repetition is directly related to the number of previous episodes of DSH. We must not allow ourselves to lose sight of the needs of those DSH patients, about half the total attending hospital, who are 'first evers' and presumably not yet committed to a recurrent pattern of DSH.

These may well be more likely to make constructive use of help and they should certainly not be excluded from therapy merely because they appear from follow-up studies to be less likely to repeat DSH in the following year or so. The 'first evers' on the whole are those that have experienced less intractible problems and have required less psychiatric treatment previously. Prevention of 'first evers' from becoming recruited to the ranks of chronic repeaters is an important therapeutic task which should not be minimized.

11.2 The Relationship Between Non-Fatal Deliberate Self-Harm and Suicide

Although we have repeatedly emphasized the clinical and demographic differences between suicides and those who survive acts of deliberate self-harm, there is of course also a close relationship between the two. We will now examine this further.

Seriousness of the episode

Whilst the majority of DSH episodes do not constitute a threat to life some of course do. Assessment of the severity of an episode of DSH is itself fraught with problems. Kessel (1965) pointed out how difficult it is to assess the degree of danger to life to which the patient, from his standpoint, has exposed himself. The amount of drug used in overdose and whether it amounts to a lethal dose is often an arbitrary matter because few patients have the necessary pharmacological knowledge about the agents involved. Recognizing these problems, Kessel devised a 'life-endangering index' which involved two independent components: the quantity of poison or drug used and the extent to which the act was concealed or disclosed. Four categories of predicted outcome were derived and the distribution of patients according to each was:
(1) Death: 19 per cent. both sexes
(2) Death probable: 11 per cent. both sexes
(3) Death unlikely: 29 per cent. males, 11 per cent. females
(4) Certain to survive: 41 per cent. males, 49 per cent. females
Essentially similar finding at a later date from Edinburgh were reported by Rosen in 1968 when 21 per cent. of episodes were found to be serious as judged by a scale which took into account medical as well as psychiatric measures (Rosen, 1970).

Suicide risk in DSH

DSH behaviour signifies a greatly increased risk of suicide at some time subsequently, probably in the order of 100 times that in the general population. During the first year after an episode it has been revealed by follow-up studies that about 1 per cent. of DSH patients kill themselves (Kreitman, 1976; Morgan *et al.*, 1976; Rosen, 1970; Tuckman and Youngman, 1963a, 1968). Long-term estimates suggest that more than 10 per cent. of DSH patients will eventually commit suicide (Dorpat and Ripley, 1967; Moss and Hamilton, 1956; Motto, 1965; Tuckman and Youngman, 1963). The greater the repetition of DSH the more likely it is that suicide will eventually occur (Ettlinger, 1964). The suicide risk amongst DSH patients seems to be age-related. Kreitman (1976) analysed annual cohorts of Edinburgh patients for 1968 and 1969 and showed that the suicide rates increased with age. It began to rise steeply in middle aged men in whom the risk was ten times greater than in younger age groups. For women the increase in risk was more gradual with increasing age and was consistently lower than for men (Table 21).

In view of the greatly increased risk of suicide which it carries, further questions concerning DSH need to be answered. Do those DSH patients who eventually kill themselves differ from the remainder in any other way and is there any practical way of differentiating them from the others? Both these points have obvious relevance to our understanding and management of DSH. Approaches to the problem of predicting suicide risk have concentrated on the seriousness of the episode and on suicidal intent, on the one hand, and differential clinical and personal characteristics, on the other. We have noted that there seems to be no consistent relationship between the seriousness of DSH episodes and the risk of subsequent non-fatal repetition. Recent reports suggest, however, that serious DSH may signify an increased risk of suicide at some time later, though earlier studies had produced equivocal findings on this point (Greer and Lee, 1967; Motto, 1965; Schmidt, O'Neal, and Robins, 1954). Using an index of both medical and psychiatric seriousness, Rosen (1970) has found in a one-year follow-up that the rate of subsequent suicide after

TABLE 21   Suicide in DSH patients (two to three-year follow-up)

Young (15–34 years)			Middle aged (35–54 years)			Older (55 years +)		
Male	Female	Total	Male	Female	Total	Male	Female	Total
0.4	1.04 (Suicide %)	0.82	4.07	1.5 (Suicide %)	2.69	7.94	3.22 (Suicide %)	5.13

Source: Kreitman, 1976.

serious episodes was greater than in non-serious ones. Tackling the problem somewhat less directly, Pallis and Sainsbury (1976) have also shown that medical seriousness of an episode of DSH correlated highly with independent measures of suicide intent using the Beck Suicide Intent Scale, and of suicide risk as measured by the validated scale of Tuckman and Youngman (1968).

Those DSH patients who subsequently kill themselves appear to differ from the remainder in terms of their individual clinical and demographic characteristics, tending to be more typical of suicides as a whole. Tuckman and Youngman (1963b, 1968) detected forty-eight subsequent deaths from suicide in 3,800 DSH patients and showed that the demographic and clinical items which were positively related to subsequent suicide were: over 45 years of age, separated, divorced or widowed, living alone, unemployed or retired, acute or chronic physical illness, medical care in the last six months, previous suicide attempts, time of attempt 6 a.m. to 6 p.m., place of attempt at home, season April to September, and presence of mental illness including behavioural disorders and alcoholism. Rosen (1970) also studied those DSH patients who actually killed themselves. He emphasized the importance of depression and insomnia as the key symptom possessed by this group and he suggested eight suicide high-risk factors: depression, insomnia, older than 40 years, married, recently separated, widowed, retired or living alone, middle class, good employment record (e.g. five years in present job).

The problem can also be examined, though less directly, by using measures of intent in DSH (Pallis and Sainsbury, 1976; Pierce, 1977): it has been shown that high suicidal intent has a strong positive association with suicide risk and seriousness of attempt, which in turn carries an increased risk of subsequent suicide. Pallis and Sainsbury (1976) demonstrated that depressive symptoms are strongly associated with high suicidal intent in DSH. The important symptoms included insomnia, pessimism regarding the future, lack of insight, weight loss, poor concentration, feeling useless and worthless, and social withdrawal. The patients at interview soon after the episode of DSH appeared discouraged, showed little eye contact and sat with shoulders slumped. This depressive symptom pattern of high suicidal intent in DSH was also demonstrated by Birtchnell and deAlarcon (1971b). It has also been pointed out (Pierce, 1977; Tuckman and Youngman, 1968) that DSH episodes other than overdoses often score highly for seriousness of suicidal intent.

A further interesting differential between patients who have a history of serious episode of DSH and those who do not concerns their personality attributes. Pallis and Birtchnell (1977) found using the Minnesota Multiphasic Personality Inventory that serious episodes were associated with patterns of intrapunitive, introspective depression whereas the non-serious showed marked personality deviance in terms of dependency, hostility, and unconventionality, especially in males. This suggested that DSH in the latter group was related to outwardly directly aggressive impulses which posed difficulties with regards to the way they related to others.

Previous DSH in suicides

The relationship between DSH and suicide may be studied from yet another angle by examining the incidence of previous non-fatal episodes in patients who eventually kill themselves: between 30 and 50 per cent. show such a history (Ovenstone, 1973; Ovenstone and Kreitman, 1974). These investigators divided suicides into those with a previous history of DSH (the P group) and those without (NP). The P group was found to be composed of sociopaths, drug addicts, and alcoholics with long histories of instability, poor response to psychiatric treatment, and living conditions of chronic personal and social disintegration; they also tended to indicate to others their intention to kill themselves. The NP group of suicides had more stable personalities, shorter periods of upset, and tended not to indicate their intentions before they killed themselves. This approach provides us with a somewhat different picture of the relationship between DSH and suicide from the one we had gained previously. Whereas studies based on the prognosis of DSH patients suggested that depressives with stable personalities contributed most to the total suicide risk, the retrospective study of actual suicides suggests that the personality disordered antisocial subgroup of DSH also contributes a considerable number of individuals to the ranks of suicides: clearly their suicide risk should not be minimized.

11.3 General and Physical Outcome

A considerable number of DSH patients at follow-up continue to show socioeconomic problems and unsettled personal relationships. We concluded from our Bristol studies that self-harm is in many cases a symptom of continuing disorder rather than a turning point in a person's life: it rarely seems to cause any radical change for the better and frequently signifies a worsening in the life situation, judging from the high incidence

138

of breakdown in relationships which continues after the event. Major physical complications are uncommon, but they cannot be regarded as insignificant, occurring as they do in persons who otherwise would be physically fit. Chronic organic brain syndromes with persistent disorder of memory may occur following head injury or cardiac arrest in severe drug overdose. Long-term residua such as peripheral nerve lesions, paraplegia due to spinal injuries, and arthritic sequelae complicating bone fractures are not rare. Chronic physical injuries complicating DSH are a serious problem: their prevalence is likely to increase progressively whilst DSH continues at its present rate, because the disabilities involved are often long lasting and sometimes permanent. The problem has been demonstrated in a most vivid way by Ettlinger (1972) who studied bodily organic and other pathological complications of DSH. Out of 221 patients 32 had some such physical complication: the impact of their disability is emphasized by the fact that the total time they spent out of work amounted to 3,760 days—just over ten years in aggregate.

12

ASSESSMENT

Wherever we are faced with a person who either has recently carried out an act of deliberate self-harm or who appears to be in imminent danger of doing so, certain basic problems in assessment arise. The first task is to carry out an evaluation of immediate risk, leading to the provision of adequate physical care in an appropriate facility: following this a definitive decision must be made with regard to the nature and setting of subsequent care. The present chapter should be read in conjunction with our earlier discussions of suicide risk assessment (Chapter 5).

12.1 Urgent Physical Assessment and Management

Most episodes of DSH lead to an urgent referral to the nearest hospital Accident and Emergency Department. Although the general practitioner is sometimes called, relatives or friends more frequently telephone for an ambulance direct without involving a medical practitioner in the home setting. In view of the fact that the type of drug used or the apparent severity of the overdose may bear little relation to the degree of underlying psychological problems, or indeed the chance of major physical complications, it is best to encourage such rapid referral. The first task is to assess the likely physical complications and where necessary initiate 'first aid' treatment.

Physical complications

Whereas the great majority of patients who have deliberately taken drug overdoses recover without the administration of special antidote preparations, some are in danger of developing physical complications, especially if basic first aid is withheld: a patient waiting at home for an ambulance may get into serious difficulties which might be avoided by the observation of certain simple principles. These are:

139

(1) *Ensure a patent airway.* A patient who becomes unconscious might develop respiratory obstruction which can be alleviated by placing him on his side in a semi-prone position, removing false teeth, clearing the mouth of vomit, and ensuring that the tongue does not fall to the back of the mouth. A short oropharyngeal tube may be useful, but it is inadvisable for untrained individuals to insert breathing aids because they might induce vomiting and so cause further respiratory obstruction. Respiratory failure is the most common and immediate cause of death in overdosage, and maintenance of adequate respiratory ventilation, if necessary with artificial respiration, is most important.

(2) *Treat cardiac arrest.* External cardiac massage may be needed in extreme and severe cases, but again basic first aid training is required before attempting it. Attention to respiratory ventilation is essential throughout.

(3) *Combat shock.* Cold cyanosed limbs with a fall in blood pressure often responds to the simple procedure of elevating the lower limbs. The patient will then be transported to hospital in the semi-prone, head-down position with the foot of the stretcher raised. When shock is severe, with systolic blood pressure less than 90 mm of mercury in persons over 50 years of age or less than 80 mm of mercury in those younger than this, a doctor might use Metaraminol 1–2 mg intravenously, repeating the dose if necessary but remembering of course that adverse reactions may ensue if the patient has been taking monoaminoxidase inhibitor drugs, particularly if they constitute the agent used for overdosage.

(4) *Use of emetic and gastric lavage.* This should be avoided if the patient has taken a caustic or corrosive poison, or petroleum distillates. At home, if the patient is fully conscious, attempts to evacuate the stomach of its contents may be worthwhile when the overdosage has been taken during the previous six to eight hours. A doctor may use 15 mg of Ipecacuahna syrup which will act in about fifteen minutes. Apomorphine or saline emetics are not now regarded as safe, the first sometimes causing prolonged vomiting and shock and the second perhaps leading to serious metabolic complications such as hypernatraemia. Gastric lavage is not recommended outside the hospital setting but once in the emergency room it is worth carrying out except of course in corrosive poisoning, because the stomach is unlikely to have been emptied completely by previously induced vomiting. Matthews and Lawson (1975) recommend gastric lavage routinely in the unconscious patient even though the time of ingestion of the drug may be unknown: it is particularly useful when carried out within four hours of the overdosage (twelve hours for tricyclic antidepressants and never too late in the case of salicylates). The usual

procedure involves placing the patient head down, having previously introduced an intratracheal cuffed tube if he is unconscious, and then passing a 30 English guage Jacque stomach tube. Recurrent gastric lavage is then carried out with 300 ml of warm water (38° C) until the washings are clear—usually a total of 5 to 10 litres is required. Skill is necessary with this procedure and makeshift attempts at gastric lavage in the home, especially with an unconscious patient, are not recommended.

Physical examination may at this time give important clues to the nature of the agent used in self-poisoning, particularly when this is not clear from the medicine bottles in the vicinity. Venepuncture sites may suggest that addictive drugs such as opiates or barbiturates are implicated. Skin blisters are useful indicators of poisoning with barbiturates, glutethimide, or tricyclic drugs. Any tablets, capsules, or empty cartons together with samples of gastric aspiration should be retained for further analysis.

Most overdose patients are admitted from hospital Accident and Emergency Departments to medical wards in order to ensure adequate physical management and to monitor the crucial period when physical complications may arise. Impaired levels of consciousness are certainly important but some drugs such as salicylates may cause serious problems of a metabolic nature without leading to drowsiness or coma. Very few specific antidotes are available and in most cases of severe overdosage the crucial factors facilitating survival are good nursing and physiotherapy. Bladder catheterization is probably undertaken too often when fundal pressure might alone suffice to ensure that the patient passes urine. Forced diuresis by intravenous infusion of fluids may be useful to accelerate elimination of a drug; occasionally more complicated procedures such as peritoneal or renal dialysis and exchange transfusions are used. A few (4 per cent.) need attention in an intensive care unit especially those who develop cardiac arrhythmias, which are a particular risk in tricyclic antidepressant poisoning, or when deep coma leads to respiratory complications such as pneumonia, commonly due to aspiration of pharyngeal and stomach contents. Maintenance of adequate respiratory ventilation is of great importance throughout. The medical problem of management of self-poisoning cannot be discussed here in more detail: they are dealt with in standard works such as that of Matthews and Lawson (1975).

We may at this point note that not all DSH patients are admitted to hospital medical wards. In Edinburgh as much as 30 per cent. of the total problem is treated at home by general practitioners. In our Bristol studies we found that about 12 per cent. returned home after being seen in hospital Accident and Emergency Departments. These patients differed from the main group of those attending with DSH in that they were mostly young females who had lacerated themselves. No doubt these would in any case be reluctant to stay in hospital and the doctor would possibly feel reassured that the full extent of physical complications had become quite clear at the time, thereby acquiescing more readily with the patient's wish to return home immediately. It is probably best to be cautious, however, in assessing the risk in these particular patients, especially when laceration is extensive, deep, in dangerous sites such as the neck or flexor aspects of the wrist, and is sufficiently severe to injure tissues such as tendons or nerves. There is evidence to suggest that non-poisoning DSH is on the whole of more serious import than is drug overdosage.

Problems in medical ward management

It is understandable that attention to physical complications is accorded paramount importance initially in the management of DSH. Only rarely is a special admissions unit available for the inpatient management of such cases, and so they are usually admitted to general medical wards: DSH patients now comprise about 20 per cent. of all acute medical admissions to hospitals in the United Kingdom (Morgan *et al.*, 1975; Smith, 1972). What problems are associated with this policy?

The task facing the medical ward is indeed a difficult one: the staff often find themselves faced with DSH patients who may be uncooperative, perhaps noisy, even aggressive, who disturb patients who are physically ill, and who may be unpredictable with regard to repeat DSH or even suicide. Often wards are short of staff and their attention to the treatment of physical illness, which they may regard as their primary task, can be severely compromised. It is perhaps not surprising therefore that attitude studies of medical ward staff have shown that most are ambivalent in their views of DSH patients (Griffin, 1975; Patel, 1975; Ramon, Bancroft, and Skrimshire, 1975). Patel's Glasgow study detected unfavourable attitudes in 25 per cent. of consultants, 44 per cent. of junior medical staff, and 40 per cent. of nurses, the majority feeling that DSH patients were unsatisfactory to treat. Ramon and her colleagues in Oxford found that nurses tended to be more accepting and sympathetic towards DSH, tending to interpret it as an escape from or manifestation of distress. Doctors there tended to see DSH as either suicidal, in which case they were sympathetic, or manipulative, in which case they felt critical and hostile. In Bristol, Griffin found no great difference between the attitudes of doctors and nurses, although junior medical staff were less sympathetic than consultants or medical students. Most felt that the general medical ward is not the best place to deal with the mental and physical problems inherent in acute DSH. If not the general medical ward, where else should the DSH patient be treated initially?

The possibility of a special unit is often mentioned: indeed in Edinburgh the advantages of such a facility appear to be unchallenged. Should the general aim be to develop such poisons treatment units? In Bristol most of the staff (69 to 85 per cent.) expressed approval of such a development and found the combination of resuscitative and psychiatric facilities an attractive prospect. On the other hand, most (52 to 94 per cent.) did not want to work in such a unit. This suggests that we should look at all the implications before assuming that a special 'overdose' unit would alleviate difficulties and not cause fresh ones. Presumably the precise issues will vary from one hospital to another but if DSH patients are to be treated separately from the main stream of general medicine we need to be sure that the unit does not carry a stigma, either from the point of view of patients or staff. Staff morale should therefore be maintained at a high level so that the unit is recognized as a sought-after training experience rather than one to be avoided. The development of such a facility would be no mean task, particularly from the financial and staffing point of view, and any compromise is likely to accentuate rather than alleviate the problems of DSH management. There is indeed much good to be found in the present system of management in the general medical ward. After all it does ensure that we all take part in the helping process and the DSH patient is not swept 'out of sight out of mind' as someone else's psychiatric problem. However, if management of DSH is to remain in the stream of general medicine then certain aspects of its management need constant careful attention. The psychiatric team must always be easily available for advice, and the relationship between the medical and psychiatric teams must be good. Ideally the ward staff will feel able to partake in the psychosocial assessment of their DSH patients, particularly interviewing relatives and friends who are not often available when the psychiatrist attends the ward. In turn the psychiatrist would want to maintain regular discussions and seminars with the ward staff. It need hardly be added that some estimates of the risk of repeat DSH, suicide, or other behaviour problems which might occur while the patient is nursed in the medical ward should be made as soon as the patient reaches hospital. If there is any doubt on this point the psychiatrist must be available to advise from the start, and he should consult with the medical and nursing staff regarding the necessary level of supervision

144

which the patient will require whilst he remains in the medical ward.

12.2 Psychological and Social Assessment

Once the physical state is judged to present no significant danger and the patient is alert, conscious, and able to reconstruct events, a formal evaluation of the factors which led to the episode of DSH is carried out with a view to deciding what management programme should be adopted. Sometimes the patient's physical state from the start presents no danger and he will be assessed in the accident and emergency room: more often he is seen in the medical ward a day or so after the episode of DSH.

The usual practice, one which has been officially recommended (Central Health Services Council, 1962; Central and Scottish Health Services Council, 1968), is to ensure that a psychiatric opinion is obtained on all DSH patients before they leave the hospital. As a result, a considerable amount of time is spent by psychiatrists in carrying out formal evaluation of these patients, though the precise arrangements between physician and psychiatrist seem to vary from one hospital to another. Our own practice is to ensure that each patient is interviewed both by a psychiatrist and social worker. These meet together in order to arrive at both a psychological and social evaluation before a final decision is reached regarding the appropriate management. This technique has been developed because it is clear that each episode of DSH presents a complex psychological and social problem: the urgent assessment of social needs such as the care and safety of young children left at home can be just as important as clinical evaluation of the patient in the hospital ward.

The assessment interview should be carried out in a quiet uninterrupted situation where the patient is able to talk at length if necessary without feeling hurried. This usually means retiring to a side room away from the setting of the open ward. Whatever may be the underlying mental illness or social crisis, the DSH patient has usually reached a point of crisis from which his view of life in general and his own situation in particular may be grossly distorted. The most common emotional concomitants are depression, anger, and frustration, often with a sense of repeated failure following which it seems pointless to persist. Such a patient may have real suicidal feelings and when faced with someone in this frame of mind it is important to remember that unless a correct approach is adopted, important clues may be missed, particularly when the patient sees the interview as an irrelevant and pointless intrusion into his private feelings and hopelessness. It is important to say little, but as soon as possible to state that one recognizes the patient's state of despair. The interview may have to move slowly as the patient comes out of his shell and feels that he is talking to someone who can perhaps understand and who by avoiding facile reassurance makes him feel that he will be taken seriously. He may not have been able to discuss his feelings with relatives for fear of 'losing face'.

Discussion of suicidal ideas must be embarked upon carefully: e.g. after commenting on the state of despair and sympathizing with the patient, noting feelings of hopelessness about the future, the conversation moves to the present and the patient is asked whether he has ever felt unable to go on with life. Following this it should be possible to discuss freely any ideas of self-destruction which the patient may have entertained. At this point the patient may show an emotional catharsis with a feeling of relief on being able to share such painful feelings. The more the clinical and socioeconomic characteristics of the patient conform to the suicide stereotype, the more one should suspect suicidal intent even when it is denied. The most important relevant personal factors are increasing age, male sex, widowed, divorced or separated, unemployed, incapacitating physical disability, especially terminal illness in the elderly, life events of a loss nature, depression and/or alcoholism, self-blame, and persistent insomnia, especially when there is a previous psychiatric history involving serious suicidal attempts. Precipitating social crises are of course also relevant to our assessment; when these have subsided, even though perhaps temporarily, then the immediate risk is less than when the episode of self-harm has alienated relatives even further, tending as they do to equate self-harm with blackmail aimed at altering their own attitudes and behaviour. The act of self-harm may give valuable clues to the true suicidal intent, which is more likely when the overdose was massive, laceration was severe, extensive, and involved vital points, or DSH was due to unusual methods such as the use of a firearm; precautions had been taken to avoid discovery and to ensure success; and the episode was well planned rather than impulsive.

DSH may of course complicate a wide variety of abnormal mental states both psychotic and otherwise. Depressive or paranoid psychosis, and even chronic alcoholism may be missed because of denial on the patient's part. This may also make assessment particularly difficult in the elderly, who often refuse to admit that they have taken other than the usual dose of night sedative. There may be no demonstrable symptoms of mental illness, though this does not mean that the patient is free from significant risk, given sufficient impulsivity of personality and a return to a social situation frought with chronic tension and interpersonal conflict, perhaps with symptomatic drinking of alcohol; then emotional tension may build up again very rapidly and lead to further DSH or even suicide. Full discussion of interpersonal and socioeconomic difficulties at the first interview is often itself therapeutic, being part of the sharing of the burden with others who want to help, and it is indeed wrong to avoid discussion of matters merely because they cannot be changed easily. As the majority of patients will have reacted to some adverse event immediately prior to the episode of DSH this aspect of evaluation is crucial.

Clearly a great deal of information from several sources should be obtained concerning each episode of DSH if its evaluation is to be adequate and thorough. A simple checklist inventory can be valuable as an aid to DSH evaluation, encouraging comprehensive data collection. It can also help to counteract a certain monotony in the hospital staff's approach to the DSH problem, one which is understandable when we pause to realize that such personnel are faced with a large number of DSH patients who stay only for short periods, certainly not long enough to get to grips with their underlying problem, and who quite often are difficult in their behaviour. Our own 'thirty questions' checklist acts as a useful discussion point between staff of all kinds (Table 22). It lists the important risk factors for repeat DSH and suicide, and the score can be assessed easily both as a visual profile as well as numerically. Such a checklist facilitates rather than replaces the usual general clinical and social assessment of each patient. Other factors may be idiosyncratic yet important in any individual case, and these can only be discovered by the use of flexible and thorough clinical interviews. Nor should a low score with regard to risk factors be used as a reason for excluding an individual from further treatment; this applies particularly to the 'first-ever' DSH patient who has not yet developed a pattern of repetitive self-harm and who may respond well to treatment.

Is a psychiatrist's opinion essential in the evaluation of DSH patients? The obvious alternative might be for physicians themselves, in cooperation with nurses and social workers, to decide what subsequent management is required, and in some areas this undoubtedly is the current approach. Lawson and Mitchell (1972) were amongst the first to suggest that early intervention by a psychiatrist is unnecessary, though they did not carry out a detailed follow-up. More recently it has been shown quite convincingly by Gardner et al. (1977), who have conducted a thorough follow-up study in Cambridge, that deliberate self-poisoning patients assessed by physicians in hospital do not carry out repeat episodes or commit suicide any more or less frequently than those assessed by psychiatrists. It should be noted, however, that these findings

TABLE 22   Risk assessment in non-fatal deliberate self-harm

Date:	Name:	Hosp. No.	No	Yes
SEX	Male			
AGE	35 years or older			
ACT OF DSH	Severity:			
	(laceration: deep/extensive/danger site/firearm)			
	(overdose: unconscious/need special aids)			
	Precaution to avoid discovery/ensure suicide			
	Premeditation (24 hours or more)			
	No obvious precipitating factors			
	Conscious suicidal intent			
SYMPTOMS	Persistent depression of mood			
PRECEDING	Self-blame			
DSH	Anger and resentment			
	Impulsive/acting-out behaviour			
	Psychotic symptoms/behaviour			
	(other than depression)			
	Serious drink problem/drug dependent			
	Longstanding serious physical			
	illness/disability			
	Persistent somatic symptoms (e.g. pain)			
SOCIAL	Recurrent crises/intractible upsetting			
	life problems			
	Lack support/no close friends/hostile			
	'key others'			
	Divorced/separated/widowed			
	Living alone/away from relatives			
	Living in city centre/social class IV, V			
PERSONAL	Suicide in first-degree relative			
HISTORY	Separation from parents for six months			
	or more before age of 15			
	(include bereavement)			
	Previous personality: impulsive/			
	acting-out/antisocial			
	Episodes of DSH in previous three months			
	Previous psychiatric treatment			
STATUS	Persistent psychiatric symptoms,			
AFTER DSH	especially depression			
	Persistent anger/resentment			
	Uncooperative/reticent/evasive			
	Continuing suicidal ideas (regret not killing self)			
	Unresolved or worsened situation			
	(social/economic/interpersonal)			
		Scores:	No	Yes

N.B. 'First-ever' overdoses respond well to intensive help.

applied in a situation where there was good communication between psychiatrists and physicians, and junior staff received adequate psychiatric tuition, especially with regard to suicide risk. Whether these findings can be generalized to situations where such conditions do not apply remains uncertain. The use of repetition and suicide rates as indices of outcome, useful though they undoubtedly are, provide only a very incomplete assessment of the total clinical picture, and we need more evaluative studies before we can accept unconditionally the conclusions of Gardner and his colleagues that physicians should decide for each of their self-poisoning patients if specialized psychiatric advice is necessary.

Workers at the Edinburgh Regional Poisoning Treatment Centre (RPTC) have long affirmed that early psychiatric assessment is beneficial (Kennedy, 1972; Kessel, 1965; Kreitman, 1977). They have demonstrated that DSH patients referred to the unit at the time of self-harm have a lower rate of repetition than do those who are not admitted to hospital, and this finding still applied when the comparison was controlled for factors, such as previous history of DSH, which have been demonstrated to denote increased risk of further episodes. Patients referred later to psychiatric clinics without initial admission to the RPTC did not appear to benefit by reduction in the incidence of subsequent DSH. This is interpreted not as an indication that psychiatric intervention is ineffective but that it came too late, usually some days or a week afterwards. Early psychotherapeutic contact may be particularly helpful because it comes at the point of crisis, before psychological defences are resumed. In summary, then, although the present evidence with regard to the value of psychiatric intervention in the early management of DSH is somewhat conflicting, there is certainly no indication that its value can be dismissed. If any service contemplates discontinuing it, this can only be justified provided very close liaison between medical and psychiatric teams is maintained.

12.3 The Choice of Treatment Programme

A minority will require psychiatric hospitalization, especially when florid mental illness and continuing suicidal ideas or a worsening social situation are present. Most are fit to take up outpatient appointments or to return to the care of their general practitioners. In practice about a fifth are admitted as psychiatric inpatients, just over half agree to attend psychiatric outpatient clinics following discharge from the medical ward, and a quarter return to the care of their general practitioners only (Morgan *et al.*, 1976). A very small number (4 per cent.) refuse inpatient psychiatric treatment and less than 1 per cent. are compulsorily admitted to hospital under a section of the Mental Health Act. Sometimes a decision regarding the best form of treatment is difficult because of the various ambiguities of the situation. It is then useful to ask for reassurance that the patient will come for help if difficulties arise before the next appointment and to ensure that discharge from hospital is mutually agreed to be a sensible step. Someone who is deeply committed to suicide may still not admit to it, but frequently a patient will discuss his feelings freely, especially when a good rapport has been established by correct interview technique. Needless to say, in any doubtful situation ease of availability of help is essential and the patient should be in no doubt where to turn for assistance if in difficulty. 'Hotlines' of this nature are not often abused, particularly when the goal of the next appointment has been mutually agreed.

Whilst it is important to admit the seriously ill, particularly those who have psychotic symptoms, for inpatient psychiatric care an immediate return home is probably the best for the majority of these patients. It can be extremely difficult to treat situational problems from a psychiatric ward, and too liberal use of hospital admission can delay rather than promote their resolution, often leading to secondary relationship problems in the ward itself. A period of care in a psychiatric day hospital may of course be a good compromise.

Occasionally it is necessary to continue treatment on an outpatient basis in spite of the presence of many risk factors: tolerating suicide risk may be indicated when repeated hospital admissions have produced no beneficial effects or perhaps even made the situation worse by reducing the patient's willingness to face problems in his life situations. Needless to say, any strategy of this kind should never be adopted out of anger on the part of the therapist and it is usually necessary to know the patient well over an extended period of time before attempting it. Regular outpatient appointments should continue to be made available to the patient.

Whatever treatment programme is agreed it is essential to ensure a quick and adequate communication with the general practitioner before the DSH patient leaves the hospital. It is not uncommon for such patients to request their general practitioner to provide further medication immediately on returning home. The doctor may find himself in serious difficulties if he has not been informed by the hospital that an overdose has recently occurred, especially when the patient chooses not to tell him. The safest way to avoid this difficulty is by the routine use of telephone calls from the hospital to general practitioner before the DSH patient is discharged.

13

MANAGEMENT AND PREVENTION

During the initial evaluation a decision has to be made regarding further management of DSH. About half of all such patients who attend hospital are discharged home without arrangements to attend a hospital clinic, less than a quarter are first admitted as inpatients directly to a psychiatric ward, and a quarter are referred directly back to the care of the general practitioner (Kreitman, 1977; Morgan et al., 1976). We must now assess the value of subsequent management and examine the various problems which arise. This will lead finally into consideration of the feasibility of primary prevention.

13.1 The Value of Psychiatric Treatment

Whilst some may feel it to be self-evident that individuals who have recently experienced a crisis in their lives will benefit from the skills of a psychiatrist and his team, the efficacy of such management is difficult to evaluate. If we confine ourselves to hospital statistics as a measurement of subsequent repetition we find that about 20 per cent. of all DSH patients who attend hospitals will repeat some form of deliberate self-harm within a year. Some studies have been content with this level of evaluation. Others have attempted to seek out the patients wherever they may be in order to obtain a more detailed comprehensive picture of the outcome: valid conclusions can only be based ultimately on comprehensive data of this kind.

An early encouraging study of DSH patients seen in the Casualty Department of a London teaching hospital found that they clearly benefited from psychiatric help. Bagley and Greer (Bagley and Greer, 1971; Greer and Bagley, 1971) followed up two groups using hospital detected repetition as well as structured interviews with the patients themselves: those who accepted psychiatric admissions and subsequently

150

continued with a course of therapy showed a lower incidence of repeat DSH than those who failed to engage in treatment, even when allowance was made for the fact that the two groups differed in certain characteristics relevant to the incidence of repetition. It appears that the benefits in the fully treated group were due entirely to the superior results in 'first evers' with no demonstrable effect in 'repeaters' nor in those regarded as having a psychopathic personality.

These findings were indeed very striking and contrasted with our own in Bristol, where it was shown that patients taken into psychiatric treatment had greater rates of subsequent DSH repetition than did those who either received very brief care or none at all, probably because of the fact that initial assessment was remarkably effective in selecting high-risk individuals for treatment (Morgan *et al.*, 1976). It is not clear why this problem of selection for treatment did not complicate the assessment of outcome in Greer and Bagley's study. In order to control for this major problem in assessing response to treatment, Kreitman and his colleagues in Edinburgh instituted an experimental after-care service for DSH patients, and those who had been admitted to the Regional Poisons Treatment Centre were randomly allocated either to the usual follow-up service or to the experimental one (Chowdhury, Hicks, and Kreitman, 1973; Kreitman, 1977). This provided intensive follow-up facilities, with home visits for those who defaulted, emergency arrangements with the help of the Samaritans organization, and continuous on-call access to the research team over a six-month period. The results with regard to DSH repetition were disappointing, no difference being found between the experimental and control groups. Marginal improvement in psychological symptoms occurred with intensive help, though a significant reduction of financial, housing, and employment problems was found. It may be relevant that only those patients who had a previous history of DSH were taken into the experimental group: we know that these have a considerably increased risk of repetition and indeed may be more difficult to treat than 'first evers'. However, this study highlights the difficulties in producing effective treatment for DSH patients and suggests that we need to develop a new type of care, perhaps one which is radically different from orthodox psychiatric and social work practice, if any major impact is to be made on the secondary prevention of DSH.

13.2 Problems of Delivering Care

The DSH problem clearly faces the treatment services with a major challenge and it is important to look at the reasons why it is so difficult to demonstrate any major impact on the situation. We need to look more closely at the way in which these patients utilize the help that is offered and the method with which they are selected for treatment.

Most studies demonstrate that only about half of DSH patients subsequently attend outpatient appointments which have been offered them when they first make contact with the hospital. No doubt this is due to several factors. There is undoubtedly unwillingness to accept the image of being a psychiatric patient, particularly when the problem is seen in terms of situational rather than personal difficulties. When resentment and hostility is marked then there will of course be reluctance to engage in subsequent treatment, whatever its nature. This probably also influences the type of help which is offered: those who show deviant behaviour are less likely to be taken on with enthusiasm in contrast to patients with depressive symptoms (Buglass and Horton, 1974), and other issues such as therapist/patient congruence, the therapist's theoretical orientation, or the patient's social class may also be relevant. Paykel *et al.* (1974) in their Newhaven study found that those patients who were young and black were more likely to drop out of subsequent outpatient treatment. Subsequent contact with services was found to be more likely if the doctor had taken the trouble to make direct contact himself with any other agency to which he might refer the patient.

There is certainly a need to develop a variety of treatment approaches in the subsequent management of DSH, taking into account the different ways in which patients perceive the help they require and their willingness to engage in treatment. A study of DSH patients in Bristol demonstrated three distinct groups according to the way in which they had used medical services previously (Turner and Morgan, 1979). The non-help seekers (41 per cent.) were those whose episodes of distress had been of acute onset and who did not see medical or other services as relevant to their problems. The general practitioner help-seekers (36 per cent.) saw their family doctor as the ideal confidant and these patients cooperated in subsequent follow-up by far the most willingly. The remainder (23 per cent.) were psychiatric help-seekers who resembled the chronically disorganized group described by Ovenstone and Kreitman (1974) and who repeat DSH in spite of continued intensive help from a variety of agencies. Advances in the treatment of DSH must take into account such variation in the way these patients are prepared to make use of help. In devising new techniques of therapy particular attention might initially be paid to those of good prognosis such as the 'first evers', because in this way new leads may be more easily detected than if more intractible problems are included to cloud the issue.

13.3 Treatment Strategies

The personal and situational problems which DSH patients face are so varied that no one form of treatment is likely to be appropriate to them all. Whatever theoretical approach is adopted, treatment must be flexible, and should take into account the specific needs and attitudes of each patient. There is a danger that such basic principles of treatment are becoming ignored in the face of the very great numbers of DSH patients who require assessment in hospital, leading to a somewhat wearied attitude of 'yet another overdose' on the part of the staff whereby each patient appears to be no different from all others.

General principles

The aim of treatment is to help the patient either to resolve his difficulties or to be able to tolerate them in a more constructive way. At all points the risk of non-fatal repetition or indeed suicide has to be taken into account and the risk factors relevant to these complications have already been discussed. Initially the patient will need a great deal of support and will show much dependence on the therapist. Treatment will work towards encouraging independence, and it is likely to be ineffective if it remains entirely a matter of doing things for or on behalf of the patient; such an approach may well encourage repetition should further crises occur. Being able to assess exactly how much a patient can and should do for himself is difficult but essential, and will depend on the early establishment of a close therapeutic relationship with full understanding of the problems involved. At times it may be necessary to allow the patient to retreat from his situation by admission to hospital; at others he should be encouraged to face his problems in the community with the therapist's support.

There is no single therapeutic setting which is appropriate to all patients. Whilst the psychiatric clinic may be acceptable to some, others such as the general practitioner help-seekers may already have a good relationship with their family doctor and would probably benefit most by referral back to him; those with alcohol problems may best be helped by specialized group support; some may well already have good relationships with social workers, probation officers, or voluntary agencies. It is essential to make direct contact, usually by telephone, before making any decision to refer a patient back to another agency. It may be that treatment by more than one therapist is required. A social worker or probation officer can offer guidance on complex social problems as well as case-work skills, and the patient may be seen in the psychiatric clinic as well. If such an arrangement is adopted, constant direct liaison between all those involved must be maintained in order to avoid ineffective fragmentation of effort.

A considerable proportion of patients have problems in their relationships with other key persons, and if possible these should be involved in therapy either on a conjoint basis or by being seen independently at first. It is particularly important to do this when the attitude of 'key others' has become hostile as a result of the episode of DSH, when without their participation the patient may quickly become the scapegoat in a complex relationship problem.

Treatment should commence as soon as possible after the episode of DSH, the therapist making contact with the patient at the time of crisis. Few patients are willing to attend subsequently unless they have already made direct contact with the person who will take on the role of therapist. It is not possible to predict how long treatment should continue and whilst some resolve their problems in a matter of weeks others will need long-term support in order to face intractable difficulties. Appointments will be set at a frequency which is mutually agreed, and it is necessary to indicate initially how help can be obtained should a crisis occur between appointments: rarely is such a 'hotline' system abused though it frequently is an effective form of support, especially in the early stages of treatment.

Physical treatments

When an overdose of prescribed medication has occurred it is necessary to review urgently whether such drugs should be continued. Frequently it is inappropriate to give further supplies, especially when there is no symptomatic indication to do so. Occasionally the patient is dependent upon psychotropic drugs and their sudden cessation, even in the case of minor tranquillizers, can lead to a further crisis involving acute anxiety and withdrawal symptoms. This is particularly liable to happen when the patient has for long been maintained on them. It may be necessary to continue the prescription, giving small amounts at frequent regular intervals during the early stages of treatment. Initial telephone contact with the usual prescriber is essential in order to coordinate this approach. It is no virtue to remove all such support by rule of thumb, and such undue firmness may be one factor leading to early default from treatment. In the case of schizophrenic psychosis it is of course necessary to continue major tranquillizers, though again with very careful supervision of the amount given and the frequency of prescription. The onset of psychotic depressive symptoms is usually an indication for readmission to hospital where physical treatment can be reviewed with some safety.

Psychotherapy

Whatever setting is chosen, psychotherapy following DSH faces us with an immense challenge. There is no single formula to be followed, if only because the needs of the patients are so varied. The adolescent girl who takes an overdose following a quarrel with her boyfriend presents a very different problem from that of the middle aged man with serious alcohol dependence, and neither may share the difficulties of the antisocial personality disorder whose life has reached a severe state of chaos.

In spite of these problems certain recurring themes in psychotherapy can be recognized and they have been emphasized by Birtchnell with reference to his work with young married individuals (Birtchnell, 1975). He points out that some kind of interpersonal crisis is the most common precipitant of DSH, reflecting difficulties in making close relationships, these presumably stemming in turn from early problems in relation to parental figures. The therapist must develop a temporary close 'holding' relationship with the patient, and often this too becomes the focus of difficulties. He has to tolerate hostility, suspicion, and testing-out behaviour: it is necessary for him to anticipate this and by recognizing it to use it constructively. It serves no purpose to dismiss such behaviour as merely indicative of 'manipulation' which should not be tolerated. His acceptance and sympathy, his commitment to therapy, and his reliability at keeping appointments himself is an important factor in encouraging the patient to continue to receive and make constructive use of help.

Very soon in treatment the problem of 'setting limits' frequently arises. An accepting therapist must also be a firm one and he has to indicate how far the patient can be allowed to regress or test out the relationship. Full discussion of further behavioural difficulties and a mutual search for the causes is of course preferable to an authoritarian defensive attitude on the part of the therapist. Whilst the search for underlying causes is essential if any radical change in behaviour is to be achieved, many patients are considerably handicapped in the degree to which they can conceptualize their problems. In all cases, however, it is necessary to discuss the act of self-harm in detail, particularly with regard to the way others react to it. So often there appears to have been little consideration of the way others may feel unfairly coerced and so become hostile, particularly when repeated episodes of DSH occur. The conjoint situation is ideal for such discussion, bringing out into the open aspects of the relationship which may not have been faced previously. The principles of conjoint therapy must of course be observed: the therapist facilitates discussion but does not take sides, he encourages the partners to face important issues rather than those which may be less painful but irrelevant, and he works towards constructive discussion rather than heated argument. The frequency with which alcohol plays a part in DSH means that it cannot be ignored in therapy. When addiction is present then it may need to be the primary focus of attention, but it is necessary to ensure that all are aware of its pharmacological effects of producing depressive mood swings as well as angry and impulsive behaviour. Repetitive self-laceration is a particularly difficult form of DSH to treat: techniques aimed at reducing the distressing subjective tension which precedes each episode may be the most fruitful approach (Gardner and Gardner, 1975; Graff and Mallin, 1967). The importance of adequate occupation and activity for self-lacerators who are confined to institutional life has also been stressed (Ballinger, 1971).

13.4 Primary Prevention

In view of the many problems which arise in trying to provide an effective form of treatment after DSH has occurred our attention must turn to the possibility of primary prevention. The principle of this approach is to provide help at an early stage, preferably before a patient has carried out a first episode of DSH or before a further crisis has developed in someone who has exhibited DSH previously. There is much to suggest that primary prevention is the most constructive approach to the DSH problem. Many crises ending in self-harm are situational and interpersonal in nature, potentially amenable to outside intervention. Once an individual has found it necessary to resort to DSH then the risk of repetition is immediately increased: DSH is in fact a self-perpetuating process increasingly difficult to influence as the number of repeats increases. The possibility of providing effective intervention before such a process develops has obvious attraction, and it may be that early help of this kind can be much more effective than after DSH which itself produces so many negative repercussions both in the patient and in the attitude of others. We have noted that of all DSH patients the 'first evers' are probably the easiest to help: the logic of primary prevention is to ensure that DSH does not occur at all. Once an individual has entered a DSH crisis there is little evidence that it can be aborted. Patients interviewed after DSH has occurred reveal that there is usually considerable resistance to seeking outside help at the time of the crisis. Such negative attitudes include a wish to die, a feeling that the problem is too personal for others to help, a search for symptomatic relief, or the need to influence others; a few feel critical of available services and their inability to help effectively (Kreitman, 1977).

Strategies in primary prevention might include increasing the availability of statutory and voluntary agencies, focusing attention on the need for early intervention in social crisis, and effectively integrating all personnel involved. It is self-evident that those at risk should know of the availability of such help and how to use it. Unfortunately there is little evidence so far to suggest that such an approach makes any impact on DSH rates in the community. At least half of DSH patients are receiving some kind of help immediately before self-harm occurs. The majority (over 80 per cent.) know of voluntary agencies such as the Samaritans yet only a small proportion (13 per cent.) seek their help. Efforts at educating the population at risk to turn more frequently to available services does not seem an attractive or cost-effective proposition. The provision of an intensive social service in the Craig Millar area of Edinburgh in which social problems abound did not produce any dramatic change in the rate of DSH in that locality: though the rates in other wards showed greater increases during the experimental period, interward comparison was difficult because of initial differences in DSH rates (Kreitman, 1977). Clearly these findings need replication in other types of city districts before we can assume that intensive community support is ineffective in the primary prevention of DSH. Central city area need particular attention. Evidence from Bristol suggests that their population underutilizes hospital psychiatric services, either by relatively low referral rates or by default from appointments (Cooksey, 1975).

Other educational approaches should be explored further. In schools basic health education could include a full discussion of deliberate self-harm; there may be anxiety on the part of education authorities that such an approach would encourage adolescents to adopt self-harming behaviour, though there is no real basis for such fears. Our work on Bristol school children's response to talks on drug addiction (Morgan and Hayward, 1976) demonstrates that informal discussions have constructive effects on children's attitudes and there is no reason to believe that the response to such an approach with regard to DSH would be any different.

We have so far ignored a vital element in the sequence of events leading to DSH and one which demands urgent further investigation: this concerns the part played by the prescription of psychotropic drugs. We have noted that the DSH 'epidemic' reflects prescribing patterns very closely both with regard to the increased fashion of prescribing psychotropic drugs and the type of drug involved. Over half of DSH patients receive psychotropic drugs by prescription shortly before self-harm occurs and they use them in deliberate self-overdosage. Naturally we must be cautious before inferring that there is a direct causal link between such prescription patterns and DSH. Kreitman (1977) has emphasized that the proportion of overdoses involving non-prescribed drugs such as salicylates and other analagesics, which are of course easily obtainable over the chemist's counter, has remained constant at about 15 per cent. of the total, indicating that their misuse in DSH has also increased considerably in recent years.

Nevertheless, the fact that so many DSH patients declare themselves to medical services shortly before an episode of self-harm constitutes a major opportunity in primary prevention. Many of them seek help from the primary health care team, and it is clear that the demands on a general practitioner make it impossible for him to spend a great deal of time discussing personal and social problems. In such a situation it is easy to see how psychotropic drugs may seem to be an easy and practical panacea. If it is impracticable for the general practitioner to provide sufficient counselling and psychotherapy for such individuals, how can this help be provided and by whom should it be carried out? Might there be a special role here for professional personnel such as health visitors or should it be provided by voluntary lay individuals? Whilst there is no doubt that psychotropic drugs can be extremely useful, it is possible that in certain people their prescription carries a serious risk of subsequent misuse by deliberate self-overdosage unless it is accompanied by adequate personal and social support. One very important task in the primary prevention of DSH must therefore be to define the personal and social characteristics of patients in whom the prescription of psychotropic drugs carries a high risk of their misuse in deliberate overdosage. These drugs should only be prescribed for such individuals with the utmost caution.

Although some aspects of primary prevention of DSH have not hitherto presented an encouraging picture, there are indeed others that give grounds for hope that a significant impact may be achieved by this approach, particularly one which places emphasis on the role of the primary health care team.

REFERENCES

Adelstein, A., and Mardon, C. (1975). Suicide 1961–74: an analysis of trends following the Suicide Act of 1961. *Population Trend*, **2**, 13–19.

Aitken, R. C. B., Buglass, D., and Kreitman, N. (1969). The changing pattern of attempted suicide in Edinburgh 1962–1967. *Brit. J. Prev. Soc. Med.*, **23**, 111–115.

Alderson, M. R. (1974). Self-poisoning—what is the future? *Lancet*, **1974**, 1040–1043.

Anderson, D. B., and McClean, L. J. (Eds.) (1971). *Identifying Suicide Potential*, Behavioural Publications, New York.

Bagley, C. (1968). The evaluation of a suicide prevention scheme by an ecological method. *Soc. Sci. Med.*, **2**, 1–14.

Bagley, C. (1975). Suicidal behaviour and suicidal ideation in adolescents: a problem for councellors in education. *Brit. J. Guidance and Counselling*, **3**, No. 2, 190–207.

Bagley, C., and Greer, S. (1971). Clinical and social predictors of repeated attempted suicide: a multivariate analysis. *Brit. J. Psychiat.*, **119**, 515–523.

Ballinger, B. R. (1971). Minor self-injury. *Brit. J. Psychiat.*, **118**, 535–538.

Bancroft, J. H. J., and Marsack, P. (1977). The repetitiveness of self-poisoning and self-injury. *Brit. J. Psychiat.*, **131**, 394–399.

Bancroft, J. H. J., Skrimshire, A. M., Reynolds, F., Simkin, S., and Smith, J. (1975). Self-poisoning and self-injury in the Oxford area. *Brit. J. Prev. Soc. Med.*, **29**, 170–177.

Bancroft, J. H. J., Skrimshire, A. M., and Simkin, S. (1976). The reasons people give for taking overdoses. *Brit. J. Psychiat.*, **128**, 538–548.

Barraclough, B. M. (1970). The effect that coroners have on the suicide rate and the open verdict rate. In E. H. Hare and J. K. Wing (Eds.), *Psychiatric Epidemiology*, Oxford University Press.

Barraclough, B. M. (1973). Differences between national suicide rates. *Brit. J. Psychiat.*, **122**, 95–96.

Barraclough, B. M. (1978a). The different incidence of suicide in Eire and in England and Wales. *Brit. J. Psychiat.*, **132**, 36–38.

Barraclough, B. M. (1978b). Reliability of violent death certificates in one coroner's district. *Brit. J. Psychiat.*, **132**, 39–41.

Barraclough, B. M., Bunch, J., Nelson, B., and Sainsbury, P. (1974). A hundred cases of suicide: clinical aspects. *Brit. J. Psychiat.*, **125**, 355–373.

159

160

Barraclough, B. M., Jennings, C., and Moss, J. R. (1977). Suicide prevention by the Samaritans. *Lancet*, **2**, 237–238.

Barraclough, B. M., Nelson, B., Bunch, J., and Sainsbury, P. (1971). Suicide and barbiturate poisoning. *J. Roy. Coll. Gen. Practit.*, **21**, 645–653.

Barraclough, B. M., and Shea, M. (1970). Suicide and Samaritan clients. *Lancet*, **2**, 868–870.

Beck, A. T., Beck, R., and Kovacs, M. (1975). Classification of suicidal behaviour: 1. quantifying intent and medical lethality. *Amer. J. Psychiat.*, **132**, 285–287.

Beck, A. T., Schuyler, D., and Herman, I. (1974). Development of suicidal intent scales. In A. T. Beck, H. L. P. Resnik, and D. J. Lettieri (Eds.), *The Predictions of Suicide*, The Charles Press Publishers, Inc., Maryland.

Beck, A. T., Weissman, A., Lester, D., and Trexler, L. (1976). Classification of suicidal behaviour: 11. Dimensions of suicidal intent. *Arch. Gen. Psychiat.*, **33**, 835–837.

Birtchnell, J. (1970a). Early parent death and mental illness. *Brit. J. Psychiat.*, **116**, 281–288.

Birtchnell, J. (1970b). The relationship between attempted suicide, depression and parent death. *Brit. J. Psychiat.*, **116**, 307–313.

Birtchnell, J. (1975). The special place of psychotherapy in the treatment of attempted suicide, and the special type of psychotherapy required. *Psychotherapy and Psychosomatics*, **25**, 3–6.

Birtchnell, J., and deAlarcon, J. (1971a). The motivation and emotional state of 91 cases of attempted suicide. *Brit. J. Med. Psychol.*, **44**, 45–52.

Birtchnell, J., and deAlarcon, J. (1971b). Depression and attempted suicide: a study of 91 cases seen in a casualty department. *Brit. J. Psychiat.*, **118**, 289–296.

Brown, G. W., Harris, T. O., and Peto, J. (1973a). Life events and psychiatric disorders. Pt. 2: Nature of causal links. *Psychological Med.*, **3**, 159–176.

Brown, G. W., Sklair, F., Harris, T. O., and Birley, J. L. T. (1973b). Live events and psychiatric disorders. Pt. 1: Some methodological issues. *Psychological Med.*, **3**, 74–87.

Buglass, D., and Horton, J. (1974). The repetition of parasuicide: a comparison of three cohorts. *Brit. J. Psychiat.*, **125**, 168–174.

Bunch, J. (1972). Recent bereavement in relation to suicide. *J. Psychosom. Res.*, **16**, 361–366.

Bunch, J., Barraclough, B. M., Nelson, B., and Sainsbury, P. (1971a). Early parental bereavement and suicide. *Social Psychiatry.*, **6**, 193–199.

Bunch, J., Barraclough, B. M., Nelson, B., and Sainsbury, P. (1971b). Suicide following bereavement of parents. *Social Psychiatry.*, **6**, 193–199.

Capstick, A. (1960). Recognition of emotional disturbance and the prevention of suicide. *Brit. Med. J.*, **1**, 1179–1182.

Cavan, R. S. (1928). *Suicide*, University of Chicago Press.

Central Health Services Council (1962). *Emergency Treatment in Hospital of Acute Poisoning*, HMSO, London.

Central and Scottish Health Services Council (1968). *Hospital Treatment of Acute Poisoning*, HMSO, London.

Choron, J. (1972). *Suicide*, Charles Scribner & Sons, New York.

Chowdhury, N., Hicks, R. C., and Kreitman, N. (1973). Evaluation of an after-care service for parasuicide ('attempted suicide') patients. *Soc. Psychiat.*, **8**, 67–81.

Clendenin, W. W., and Murphy, G. E. (1971). Wrist cutting. *Arch. Gen. Psychiat.*, **25**, 465–469.

Cooksey, G. D. (1975). A demographic analysis of psychiatric outpatients and non-attenders: its relevance to planning psychiatric services in an area of urban deprivation. Medical Student Project, University of Bristol, England.

Diggory, J. C. (1974). Predicting suicide: will-o-the-wisp or reasonable challenge? In A. T. Beck, H. L. P. Resnik, and D. J. Lettieri (Eds.), *The Predictions of Suicide*, The Charles Press Publishers, Inc., Maryland.

Dorpat, T. L., and Ripley, H. S. (1960). A study of suicide in the Seattle area. *Comprehensive Psychiat.*, **1**, 349–359.

Dorpat, T. L., and Ripley, H. S. (1967). The relationship between attempted suicide and completed suicide. *Comprehensive Psychiat.*, **8**, 74–79.

Douglas, J. D. (1967). *The Social Meaning of Suicide*. Princeton University Press.

Dublin, L. I. (1963). *Suicide: A Sociological and Statistical Study*, Ronald Press, New York.

Durkheim, E. (1951). *Suicide: A Study in Sociology*, J. A. Spaulding and G. Simpson (Trans.). Glencoe, Illinois.

Ettlinger, R. (1964). Suicides in a group of patients who had previously attempted suicide. *Acta Psychiat. Scand.* **40**, 363.

Ettlinger, R. (1972). *Somatic Sequelae in Suicide and Attempted Suicide*, Nordiska Cokhandelnsforleg., Stockholm.

Evans, J. G. (1967). Deliberate poisoning in the Oxford area. *Brit. J. Prev. Soc. Med.*, **21**, 97–107.

Farberow, N. L. (1957). Summary. In E. S. Shneidman and N. L. Farberow (Eds.), *Clues to Suicide*, McGraw-Hill, New York, Toronto, London. pp. 290–321.

Farberow, N. L., and Shneidman, E. S. (1961). *The Cry for Help*, McGraw-Hill, New York.

Farberow, N. L., Shneidman, E. S., and Neuringer, C. (1966). Case history and hospitalisation factors in suicides of neurotic hospital patients. *J. Nerv. Ment. Dis.*, **142**, 32–44.

Faris, R. E. L. (1948). *Social Disorganisation*, Ronald Press Co., New York.

Flood, R. A., and Seager, C. P. (1968). Case records of patients who committed suicide. *Brit. J. Psychiat.*, **114**, 443–450.

Fox, R. (1976). Suicide and its prevention in Britain. In E. S. Shneidman (Ed.), *Suicidology: Contemporary Developments*, Grune and Stratton, New York.

Fremming, K. H. (1951). *The Expectation of Mental Infirmity in a Sample of the Danish Population*, Cassell, London.

Gardner, A. R., and Gardner, A. J. (1975). Self-mutilation, obsessionality and narcissism. *Brit. J. Psychiat.*, **127**, 127–132.

Gardner, E. A., Bahn, A. K., and Mack, M. (1964). Suicide and psychiatric care in the ageing. *Arch. Gen. Psychiat.*, **10**, 547.

Gardner, R., Hanka, R., O'Brien, V. C., Page, A. J. F., and Rees, R. (1977). Psychological and social evaluation in cases of deliberate self-poisoning admitted to a general hospital. *Brit. Med. J.*, **2**, 1567–1570.

Ghodse, A. H. (1976). Drug problems dealt with by 62 London casualty departments: a preliminary report. *Brit. J. Prev. Soc. Med.*, **30**, 251–256.

Graff, H., and Mallin, R. (1967). The syndrome of the wrist cutter. *Amer. J. Psychiat.*, **124**, 36–42.

Graham, J. D. P., and Hitchens, R. A. N. (1967). Acute poisoning and its prevention. *Brit. J. Prev. Soc. Med.*, **21**, 108–114.

Greer, S., and Bagley, C. (1971). Effects of psychiatric intervention in attempted suicide: a controlled study. *Brit. Med. J.*, **1**, 310–312.

Greer, S., and Lee, H. A. (1967). Subsequent progress of potentially lethal attempted suicides. *Acta Psychiat. Scand.*, **43**, 361–371.

Griffin, N. V. (1975). Attitudes of hospital staff to self-harm patients in Bristol. Elective Medical Student Project, University of Bristol.

Helgason, T. (1964). The epidemiology of mental disease in Iceland. *Acta Psychiat. Scand.*, Suppl. 173.

Hendin, H. (1969). *Black Suicide*, Basic Books Inc., New York.

Holding, T. A., and Barraclough, B. M. (1975). Psychiatric morbidity in a sample of a London coroner's open verdicts. *Brit. J. Psychiat.*, **127**, 133–143.

Holding, T. A., Buglass, D., Duffy, J. C., and Kreitman, N. (1977). Parasuicide in Edinburgh—a seven year review, 1968–1974. *Brit. J. Psychiat.*, **130**, 534–543.

Jacobs, S. C., Prusoff, A. A., and Paykel, E. S. (1974). Recent life events in schizophrenia and depression. *Psychological Med.*, **4**, 444–453.

James, I. P. (1966). Blood alcohol levels following successful suicide. *Quart. J. Stud. Alcohol*, **27**, 23–29.

James, I. P. (1967). Suicide and mortality among heroin addicts in Britain. *Brit. J. Addictions*, **62**, 391–398.

James, I. P. (1975). *Compulsive Autotomy*. Paper read at the Prison Medical Service Annual Clinical Conference, London, 1975.

Jennings, C., Barraclough, B. M., and Moss, J. R. (1978). Have the Samaritans lowered the suicide rate? A controlled study. *Psychol. Med.*, **8**, 413–422.

Kastenbaum, R. (1976). Suicide as a preferred way of death. In E. S. Shneidman (Ed.), *Suicidology: Contemporary Developments*, Grune and Stratton, New York.

Kennedy, P. (1972). Efficacy of a regional poisoning treatment centre in preventing further suicidal behaviour. *Brit. Med. J.*, **4**, 255–257.

Kennedy, P., and Kreitman, N. (1973). An epidemiological survey of parasuicide ('attempted suicide') in general practice. *Brit. J. Psychiat.*, **123**, 23–34.

Kessel, N. (1965). Self-poisoning. *Brit. Med. J.*, **2**, 1265–1270, 1336–1340.

Kessel, N., and Grossman, G. (1961). Suicide in alcoholics. *Brit. Med. J.*, **2**, 1671–1672.

Kiev, A. (1971). Suicide prevention. In D. B. Anderson and L. J. McClean (Eds.), *Identifying Suicidal Potential*, Behavioural Publications, New York. pp. 3–13.

Kiev, A. (1976). Crisis intervention and suicide prevention. In E. S. Shneidman (Ed.), *Suicidology: Contemporary Developments*, Grune and Stratton, New York. pp. 454–478.

Kreitman, N. (1976). Age and parasuicide ('attempted suicide'). *Psychological Med.*, **6**, 113–121.

Kreitman, N. (Ed.) (1977). *Parasuicide*, John Wiley, London.

Kreitman, N., Smith, P., and Eng-Seong Tan (1969). Attempted suicide in social networks. *Brit. J. Prev. Soc. Med.*, **23**, 116–123.

Kreitman, N., Smith, P., Eng-Seong Tan (1970). Attempted suicide as language: an empirical study. *Brit. J. Psychiat.*, **116**, 465–473.

Lancet (1974). Annotation: self-injury. **2**, 936–937.

Lancet (1977). Drug induced depression. Leading article, **2**, 1333–1334.

Lancet (1978). Suicide and the Samaritans. Leading article, **2**, 772.

Lawson, A. A. H., and Mitchell, I. (1972). Patients with acute poisoning in a general medical unit. *Brit. Med. J.*, **4**, 153–156.

Lester, D. (1972). *Why People Kill Themselves*, Charles C. Thomas, Springfield, Illinois.

Lester, D. (1974). Demographic versus clinical predictors of suicidal behaviour. In A. T. Beck, H. L. P. Resnick, and D. J. Lettieri (Eds.), *The Predictions of Suicide*, The Charles Press Publishers, Inc., Maryland.

Linden, L. L., and Breed, W. (1976). The demographic epidemiology of suicide. In E. S. Shneidman (Ed.), *Suicidology: Contemporary Developments*, Grune and Stratton, New York.

Litman, R. E., Curphey, T., Shneidman, E. S., Farberow, N. L., and Tarachnik, N. (1963). The psychological autopsy of equivocal deaths. *J. Amer. Med. Ass.*, **184**, 924–929.

Litman, R. E., and Farberow, N. L. (1961). Emergency evaluation of self-destructive potentiality. In D. L. Farberow and E. S. Shneidman (Eds.), *The Cry for Help*, McGraw-Hill, New York.

Litman, R. E., Farberow, N. L., Wold, C. I., and Brown, T. R. (1974). Prediction models of suicidal behaviour. In A. T. Beck, H. L. P. Resnick, and D. J. Lettieri (Eds.), *The Predictions of Suicide*, The Charles Press Publishers, Inc., Maryland.

Litman, R. E., and Wold, C. I. (1976). Beyond crisis intervention. In E. S. Shneidman (Ed.), *Suicidology: Contemporary Developments*, Grune and Stratton, New York.

Lönnqvist, J. (1977). Suicide in Helsinki: an epidemiological and social psychiatric study of records in Helsinki, 1960–61 and 1970–71. Monograph of Psychiatrica Fennica. Ed. K. A. Achté. Helsinki Central Hospital.

McCarthy, P. D., and Walsh, D. (1975). Suicide in Dublin: I. The under-reporting of suicide and the consequences for national statistics. *Brit. J. Psychiat.*, **126**, 301–308.

McCulloch, J., Philip, A. E., and Carstairs, G. M. (1967). The ecology of suicidal behaviour. *Brit. J. Psychiat.*, **113**, 313–319.

McKerracher, D. W., Loughnane, T., and Watson, R. A. (1968). Self-mutilation in female psychopaths. *Brit. J. Psychiat.*, **114**, 829–832.

McMahon, B., and Pugh, T. F. (1965). Suicide in the widowed. *Amer. J. Epidemiology*, **81**, 23–31.

Maris, R. (1971). Some neglected dimensions of self-destruction in the megalopolis. In D. B. Anderson and L. J. McClean (Eds.), *Identifying Suicide Potential*, Behavioural Publications, New York.

Matthews, H., and Lawson, A. A. H. (1975). *Treatment of Common Acute Poisonings*, 3rd ed. Churchill Livingstone, Edinburgh.

Mayfield, E., and Montgomery, D. (1972). Alcoholism, alcohol intoxication and

164

suicide attempts. *Arch. Gen. Psychiat.*, **27**, 349–353.

Menninger, K. (1938). *Man Against Himself*, Harcourt, Brace and World, Inc., New York.

Mezey, A. G. (1960). Personal background, emigration and mental disorder in Hungarian refugees. *J. Ment. Sci.*, **106**, 618.

Micic, S., Rajs, J., and Pandurovic, S. (1967). 11 suicidionei minorenni. Osservazioni su autopsie eseguite a Belgrado nel perlodo, 1953–1962. *Minerva Pediat.*, **19**, 255.

MIND (1975). *A Human Condition: The Mental Health Act from 1959 to 1975: Observation, Analysis and Proposals for Reform*, Anne Ross (Ed.). National Association of Mental Health, London.

Morgan, H. G., Barton, J., Pottle, S. Pocock, H., and Burns-Cox, C. J. (1976). Deliberate self-harm: a Follow-up study of 279 patients. *Brit. J. Psychiat.*, **128**, 361–368.

Morgan, H. G., Burns-Cox, C. J., Pocock, H., and Pottle, S. (1975). Deliberate self-harm: clinical and socioeconomic characteristics of 368 patients. *Brit. J. Psychiat.*, **127**, 564–574.

Morgan, H. G., and Hayward, A. (1976). The effects of drug talks to schools children. *Brit. J. Addiction*, **71**, 101–104.

Morgan, H. G., Pocock, H., and Pottle, S. (1975). The urban distribution of non-fatal deliberate self-harm. *Brit. J. Psychiat.*, **126**, 319–328.

Moss, L. M., and Hamilton, D. M. (1956). The psychotherapy of the suicidal patient. *Amer. J. Psychiat.*, **112**, 814–820.

Motto, J. A. (1965). Suicide attempts—a longitudinal view. *Arch. Gen. Psychiat.*, **13**, 516–520.

Mowrer, E. R. (1942). *Disorganisation—Personal and Social*, Lippincott, New York.

Murphy, G. E., and Robins, E. (1967). Social factors in suicide. *J. Amer. Med. Ass.*, **199**, 303–308.

Neuringer, C. (1961). Dichotomous evaluations in suicidal individuals. *J. Consult. Clin. Psychol.*, **25**, 445–449.

Neuringer, C. (1964). Rigid thinking in suicidal individuals. *J. Consult. Clin. Psychol.*, **28**, 54–58.

Neuringer, C. (1976). Current developments in the study of suicidal thinking. In E. S. Shneidman (Ed.), *Suicidology: Contemporary Developments*, Grune and Stratton, New York and London. pp. 229–251.

Norvig, J., and Nielsen, B. (1956). A follow-up study of 221 alcoholic addicts in Denmark. *Quart. J. stud. Alc.*, **17**, 633.

Osmond, H., and Hoffer, A. (1967). Schizophrenia and suicide. *J. Schizophrenia*, **1**, 54.

Ovenstone, I. M. K. (1973). Spectrum of suicidal behaviour in Edinburgh. *Brit. J. Prev. Soc. Med.*, **27**, 27–35.

Ovenstone, I. M. K., and Kreitman, N. (1974). Two syndromes of suicide. *Brit. J. Psychiat.*, **124**, 336–345.

Pallis, D. J., and Birtchnell, J. (1977). Seriousness of suicide attempt in relation to personality. *Brit. J. Psychiat.*, **130**, 253–260.

Pallis, D. J., and Sainsbury, P. (1976). The value of assessing intent in attempted suicide. *Psychol. Med.*, **6**, 487.

Patel, A. R. (1975). Attitudes towards self-poisoning. *Brit. Med. J.*, **2**, 426–430.

Paykel, E. S., Hallowell, C., Dressler, D. M., Shapiro, D. L., and Weissman, M. M. (1974). Treatment of suicide attempts. *Arch. Gen. Psychiat.*, **31**, 487–491.

Paykel, E. S., Prusoff, B. A., and Myers, J. K. (1975). Suicide attempts and recent life events: a controlled comparison. *Arch. Gen. Psychiat.*, **32**, 327–333.

Pierce, D. W. (1977). Suicidal intent in self-injury. *Brit. J. Psychiat.*, **130**, 377–385.

Ping Nie Pao (1969). The syndrome of delicate wrist cutting. *Brit. J. Med. Psychol.*, **42**, 195–205.

Pitts, F. N. Jr., and Winokur, G. (1964). Affective disorders. III: Diagnostic correlates and incidence of suicide. *J. Nerv. Ment. Dis.*, **139**, 176.

Podvoll, E. M. (1969). Self-mutilation within a hospital setting: a study of identity and social compliance. *Brit. J. Med. Psychol.*, **42**, 213–221.

Pokorny, A. D. (1960). Characteristics of 44 patients who subsequently committed suicide. *Arch. Gen. Psychiat.*, **2**, 314–323.

Pokorny, A. D. (1964). Suicide rates in various psychiatric disorders. *J. Nerv. Ment. Dis.*, **139**, 499.

Ramon, S., Bancroft, J. H. J., and Skrimshire, A. (1975). Attitudes towards self-poisoning among physicians and nurses in a general hospital. *Brit. J. Psychiat.*, **127**, 257–264.

Registrar General (1967). *Statistics review.* Pt. II: *Commentary.* HMSO, London.

Roberts, F. J., and Hooper, D. F. (1969). The natural history of attempted suicide in Bristol. *Brit. J. Med. Psychol.*, **42**, 303–311.

Robins, E., Murphy, G. E., Wilkinson, R. H., Gassner, S., and Kayes, J. (1959a). Some clinical considerations in the prevention of suicide based on a study of 134 successful suicides. *Amer. J. Public Health*, **49**, 888–898.

Robins, E., Gassner, S., Kayes, J., Wilkinson, R. H., and Murphy, G. E. (1959b) The communication of suicidal intent: a study of 134 cases of successful (completed) suicide. *Amer. J. Psychiat.*, **115**, 724–733.

Rosen, D. H. (1970). The serious suicide attempt: epidemiological and follow-up study of 886 patients. *Amer. J. Psychiat.*, **127**, 764–770.

Rosen, G. (1971). History in the study of suicide. *Psychol. Med.*, **1**, 267–285.

Rowland, A. J. (1975). Personal Communication.

Royal College of Psychiatrists (1977). The Royal College of Psychiatrists' Memorandum on the use of electroconvulsive therapy. *Brit. J. Psychiat.*, **131**, 261–272.

Russell, Bertrand (1946). Quotation from Plato's Phaedo. In *History of Western Philosophy.* Allen and Unwin, London. p. 155.

Ryback, R. S. (1971). Self-mutilation during alcohol amnesia: report of a case. *Brit. J. Psychiat.*, **118**, 533–534.

Sainsbury, P. (1955). *Suicide in London*, Maudsley Monograph No. 1 Chapman and Hall, London.

Sainsbury, P. (1962). Suicide in later life. *Geront. Clin.*, **4**, 161–170.

Sainsbury, P. (1963). Social and epidemiological aspects of suicide in the aged. In R. H. Williams, (Ed.), *Process of Aging*, Vol. II, Atherton Press, New York.

Sainsbury, P. (1968). Suicide and depression. In A. Coppen and A. Walk (Eds.),

Recent Developments in Affective Disorders, British Journal of Psychiatry Special Publication No. 2. Headley Bros., Ashford, Kent.

Sainsbury, P. (1973). Suicide: opinions and facts. *Proc. Roy. Soc. Med.*, **66**, 579–587.

Sainsbury, P. (1975). Suicide. In K. P. Kisker, J. E. Meyer, C. Müller, and E. Ströngren (Eds.), *Psychiatrie der Gegenwart*, Vol. 3. Springer-Verlag, Berlin and Heidelberg.

Sainsbury, P., and Barraclough, B. W. (1968). Differences between suicide rates. *Nature (London)*, **220**, 1252.

Sawyer, J., Sudak, H., and Hall, S. (1972). A follow-up study of 53 suicides known to a suicide prevention centre. *Life-Threatening Behaviour*, **2**, 227–238.

Schmid, C. F. (1928). *Suicide in Seattle, 1914–1925: An Ecological and Behaviouristic Study*. University of Washington Press, Seattle, Washington.

Schmid, C. F. (1937). *Social Saga of Two Cities: An Ecological and Statistical Study of Social Trends in Minneapolis and St. Paul, Minneapolis*. Minneapolis Council of Social Agencies Monograph No. 1., pp. 370–380.

Schmidt, E., O'Neal, P., and Robins, E. (1954). Evaluation of suicidal attempts as a guide to therapy. *J.A.M.A.*, **155**, 549–557.

Seager, C. P., and Flood, R. A. (1965). Suicide in Bristol. *Brit. J. Psychiat.*, **111**, 919–932.

Shaffer, D. (1974). Suicide in childhood and early adolescence. *J. Child Psychology and Psychiatry*, **15**, 275–291.

Shneidman, E. S. (1976). Suicide notes reconsidered. In E. S. Shneidman (Ed.), *Suicidology: Contemporary Developments*, Grune and Stratton, New York. pp. 253–278.

Shneidman, E. S., and Farberow, N. L. (1957). Comparison between genuine and simulated suicide notes by means of Mowrer's DRQ. *J. Gen. Psychol.*, **56**, 251–256.

Shneidman, E. S., Farberow, N. L., and Leonard, D. (1962). Suicide: evaluation and treatment of suicidal risk among schizophrenic patients in psychiatric hospitals. *Med. Bull. Veterans' Adm. (Wash.)*, **1962**, No. 8.

Shneidman, E. S., Farberow, N. L., and Litman, R. E. (1961). The suicide prevention centre. In N. L. Farberow and E. S. Shneidman (Eds.), *The Cry for Help*, McGraw-Hill, New York. pp. 6–18.

Smith, A. J. (1972). Self-poisoning with drugs: a worsening situation. *Brit. Med. J.*, **4**, 157–159.

Smith, J. S., and Davison, K. (1971). Changes in the pattern of admission for attempted suicide in Newcastle-upon-Tyne during the 1960s. *Brit. Med. J.*, **4**, 412–415.

Stengel, E. (1952) Enquires into attempted suicide. *Proc. Roy. Soc. Med.*, **45**, 613–620.

Stengel, I., and Cook, N. G. (1958). *Attempted Suicide: Its Social Significance and Effects*, Maudsley Monograph No. 4. Chapman and Hall, London.

Swanson, W. C., and Breed, W. (1976). Black suicide in New Orleans. In E. S. Shneidman (Ed.), *Suicidology: Contemporary Developments*, Grune and Stratton, New York.

Tabachnick, N. (1970). Suicide prevention center: University of California, Los Angeles. *Calif. Med.*, **112**, 1–8.

Taylor, D. C. (1972). Mental state and temporal lobe epilepsy—a correlative account of 100 patients treated surgically. *Epilepsia*, **13**, 727–765.

Temoche, A., Pugh, H. F., and MacMahon, B. (1964). Suicide rates among current and former mental institution patients. *J. Nerv. and Ment. Dis.*, **138**, 124–130.

Tripodes, P. (1976). Reasoning patterns in suicide notes. In E. S. Shneidman (Ed.), *Suicidology: Contemporary Developments*, Grune and Stratton, New York. pp. 203–228.

Tuckman, J., and Youngman, W. F. (1963a). Suicide among persons attempting suicide. *Publ. Health Report*, **78**, 585–587.

Tuckman, J., and Youngman, W. F. (1963b). Identifying suicide risk groups among attempted suicides. *Publ. Health Report*, **78**, 763–766.

Tuckman, J., and Youngman, W. F. (1968). A scale for assessing suicide risk of attempted suicide. *J. Clin. Psychol.*, **24**, 17–19.

Tuckman, J., Youngman, W. F., and Leifer, B. (1966). Suicide and family disorganisation. *Inst. J. Soc. Psychiat.*, **12**, 187.

Turner, R. J., and Morgan, H. G. (1979). Patterns of health care in non-fatal deliberate self-harm. In Press. *Psychol. Med.*

Varah, C. (1973). *Samaritans in the '70s*, Constable, London.

Walker, W. Lumsden (1978). Personal communication.

Weiss, J. M. A. (1954). Suicide: an epidemiological analysis. Psychiat. *Quart.*, **28**, 225–252.

Weiss, J. M. A. (1974). Suicide. In *American Handbook of Psychiatry*, 2nd ed., **111**, 743–765.

Weissman, M. M. (1974). The epidemiology of suicide attempts, 1960–1971. *Arch. Gen. Psychiat.*, **30**, 737–746.

Wexler, L., Weissman, M. M., and Kasl, S. V. (1978). Suicide attempts 1970–1975: updating a United States study. *Brit. J. Psychiat.*, **132**, 180–185.

Whitlock, F. A. (1973a). Suicide in England and Wales, 1959–63. Part 1: the county boroughs. *Psychol. Med.*, **3**, 350–365.

Whitlock, F. A. (1973b). Suicide in England and Wales, 1959–63. Part 2: London *Psychol. Med.*, **3**, 411–420.

Whitlock, F. A., and Evans, L. E. J. (1978). Drugs and Depression. *Drugs*, **15**, 53–71.

Whitlock, F. A., and Schapira, K. (1967). Attempted suicide in Newcastle-upon-Tyne. *Brit. J. Psychiat.*, **113**, 423–434.

Wilkins, J. (1970). A follow-up study of those who called at a suicide prevention centre. *Amer. J. Psychiat.*, **127**, 155–161.

Wilson, D. (1869). *Chatterton: a Biographical Study*, Macmillan and Co., London.

World Health Organisation (1961). Suicide: deaths by months, according to sex. *Epidem. Vital Statist. Rep.*, **14**, 534–538.

World Health Organisation (1968a). Mortality statistics. *World Health Statis. Rep.*, **21**, 365.

World Health Organisation (1968b). *Prevention of Suicide*. Public Health Paper No. 35. Geneva.

World Health Organisation (1974). *Suicide and Attempted Suicide*. Public Health Paper No. 58. Eileen Brooke.

INDEX

169